T0380682

# THE NEW WORD FOR THE NEW AGE

## A BEGINNER'S PRIMER

### AMAZING INFORMATION FROM THE HIGHER SELF

Charles E. Zecher

BALBOA.PRESS
A DIVISION OF HAY HOUSE

Balboa Press books may be ordered through booksellers or by contacting:

Balboa Press
A Division of Hay House
1663 Liberty Drive
Bloomington, IN 47403
www.balboapress.com
844-682-1282



Print information available on the last page.

ISBN: 978-1-9822-7359-0 (sc)
ISBN: 978-1-9822-7360-6 (e)

Balboa Press rev. date: 09/03/2021

# ABOUT THE AUTHOR

The author is an extremely proficient user of the pendulum who channels his higher self. He has been a student of metaphysics, Edgar Cayce readings, Theosophy and spiritism nearly sixty years.

# FOREWORD

The information provided in this book came from thousands of questions I have asked of my higher self through the use of a pendulum.

The use of the pendulum can be an extremely useful tool in accessing the higher self. All higher selves are connected to one another. When the pendulum user connects with his higher self, he is also connecting with the higher selves of all others. He can retrieve information from anyone's higher self.

Psychics are people who can channel information from their higher selves without the use of a tool. Some psychics are able to provide more accurate information than others because of the level of evolution of their soul and consequently the level of their higher self. The same is true regarding the user of the pendulum.

There were many sources for the questions asked: anything I could think of; information I had included in books I have written; ideas that came from reading other printed materials; ideas from watching You Tube or from watching a few television programs and suggestions from other people.

As you peruse the various chapters, you will notice that there is no limit to the knowledge that can be received.

Before you read Part One, you may want to glance at Part Four. Awareness of the Definition of Terms may facilitate your understanding of new concepts.

# INTRODUCTION

The human soul is dynamic, always changing by the input of the thoughts, words and actions of the individual. Some souls are of more highly evolved than others depending on the amount and kind of input. Souls with self-centered or negative input are not as evolved as those with a greater degree of regard for other people and more positive input.

The deepest level of human consciousness from which information can be received is the higher self. The higher self can be defined as the elements and aspects of the soul that are necessary for the current incarnation. All knowledge accessible to a person is stored there. When the soul is of a higher level, the level of the higher self and the level of information that can be retrieved from it is more extensive and accurate.

The only area that cannot be foreseen with one hundred percent accuracy is when information is sought based on a person's future actions. This is because humans have been endowed with free will. Free will means a person's desires and subsequent actions. Predictions of future actions can only based on how the individual reacted to similar past actions.

No one else can overrule a person's desires. Others may create situations in which the individual is unable to follow through on his desires but only the person himself can change his desires. If others could control a person's will, it would not be free will.

Sometimes similar information may appear in different sections of the book if they are relevant to those sections. As you read, keep in mind that future events cannot be predicted with 100 percent accuracy when they involve the exercise of a person's free will.

# IN REMBRANCE OF SONDRA PERLIN ZECHER

My wife, Sondra, made her transition to the spirit world approximately eighteen months before this book was published. Much credit should be given to her, however, for her contributions to the publication of this book.

Prior to her death, Sondra and I were the sponsors of the Coral Springs Metaphysical Group. Several different types of meetings were held each month. Sondra was both a psychic and a medium. At one of the monthly meetings Sondra would do deep trance channeling.

During those sessions, she was able to channel her spirit guide. Anybody present was able to ask the guide whatever questions they chose to ask and the spirit guide would speak through Sondra. The majority of the questions asked by the participants pertained to their personal situations.

As for myself, I prepared approximately thirty questions of a metaphysical nature that could be of interest to those present. Over a period of several years, approximately 2600 questions that I prepared were answered. Those questions and answers provided by the spirit guide supplied much of the material for the content of Part One in this book.

In addition to her contributions to Part One, some of Sondra's previous writings appear in Part Three.

# CONTENTS

## Part One

## THE PENDULUM PROVIDES INFORMATION

## Part Two

## CHANNELED AND ADDITIONAL INFORMATION



## Part Three

## SONDRA

## Part Four

## ABOUT THE PENDULUM



## Part Five

## EXPLANATION OF TERMS

Masters
Medium
Mental world
Nephilim giants
New Age
Niburu
One World Order
Priory of Sion
Reincarnation
Soul
Spirit
Spirit guide
Spirit world
Split Soul
Star child
Stargate
Sumer
Theosophy
Tiamat
Walk-ins
Walk-outs
Watchers

# Part One

# THE PENDULUM PROVIDES INFORMATION

# ANCIENT HISTORY

## Atlantis and Lemuria

Atlantis was a continent that emerged approximately 285,000 years ago and was first inhabited by human extraterrestrials 88,000 years ago. The descendants of the extraterrestrials became the inhabitants of the continent.

Atlantis was located in the central part the Atlantic Ocean, east of what is now the United States. When it was its largest size, it was about the same size as Australia.

The Atlanteans were a hybrid race of the descendants of extraterrestrials who mated with Earth humans and colonized the earth. Many of the oriental people alive today are reincarnations of the Atlanteans. They were not physically different from us to the point that we could see that they were not like modern humans. They were beautiful human beings.

There were different human races, such as those now on Earth, at the time of Atlantis. The American Indians were the closest to what Atlanteans looked like, with red skin.

The Atlanteans had advanced technologies and they were interested in the mechanics of building. They and humans of long ago had medical knowledge that exceeded that which we have today.

They had air travel but they did not need ground vehicles for transportation. Flying machines powered by crystals were much easier. The architecture of the homes in Atlantis was similar to that of ancient Greece or Rome with big wide spaces and there was a variety of structures for individual divisions inside.

Some of the crystals that the Atlanteans used to transmit energy are still in operation under the sea today in the area of the Bermuda Triangle as well as in other places. They are the cause of the disappearance of planes and ships. The role of the ancient Druids in England was to preserve the Atlantean knowledge

The Atlanteans were highly involved in technology, which eventually caused the destruction of the continent. Initially there were several land masses that comprised Atlantis. There were no natural Earth changes that affected the lands of Atlantis other than the final Earth shift which sent the major part of the continent to become what is now Antarctica. Earth pole shifts have been caused by nuclear explosions but explosions are not what caused Atlantis to become Antarctica. An earthquake is what caused Atlantis to shift and become what is now Antarctica.

The land masses of Atlantis were broken up into smaller islands by the use of their technology to probe deep into the core of the earth.

The last part of Atlantis disappeared 10,173 years ago. The Atlanteans were aware that the island was going to disappear; so its population was scattered throughout the world in advance to different parts of the world in varying numbers. The greatest number of people went to Sumer in what is now southern Iraq but some went directly to Egypt while others migrated from Sumer to Egypt. Others scattered through the world including to what is now the United States. There were other Homosapiens wherever they went. The Atlanteans easily blended in with them. They did not play a role in Africa which was then a cradle of civilization.

They practiced religion, not much different from the basic tenets of most religions today. They did not believe in what we call Christs. Religion was not used for comfort as it is today but rather used to keep society in line. They had something comparable to the Judeo-Christian Ten Commandments. There were no places of worship. There was only one religion and it was not monotheistic. The Atlanteans worshipped many gods. Their religion was disseminated throughout the world and many aspects of it are incorporated in religions today including Judaism, Christianity and Islam.

Atlantis and Lemuria never coexisted. The Lemurian civilization began 730,000 years ago and ended 477,721 years ago. The Hawaiian Islands were once part of Lemuria. There are remnants of the Lemurian civilization that are on Earth today; including the statues on Easter Island. Some Polynesians are the physical descendants of the Lemurians. They resemble the ancient Lemurians. Floods destroyed the continent of Lemuria. Their bodies were as dense as our bodies are now but there was also a time in the earlier part of their civilization that they were lighter in the fourth density.

There were 29,976 advanced human civilizations on Earth prior to Lemuria and Atlantis. In addition to Atlantis and Lemuria, there is physical evidence of other past civilizations comparable to Atlantis or Lemuria. One of those past civilizations that predate Lemuria is submersed off the coast of Cuba.

## Noah and the great flood

The land masses of this world before the Great Flood 10,321 years ago were considerably different from the way they are today. Ocean levels were much lower than they are now, thus causing many coastal areas to be inundated by the flood. The total land mass of the earth was greater than it is now. The Nile River flowed into the

Atlantic Ocean at the time of Atlantis. India and the area around it were not connected to the rest of Asia. The cause of the Great Flood that is mentioned in the Bible and in the lore of other ancient civilizations throughout the world was the accumulation of weather that had formed.

There are monuments on Earth today that predate the Great Flood, such as the Sphinx. The building of the Sphinx began 93,780 years ago, before the Atlantean civilization. There wasn't only one Great Flood. There were many floods over and over and over. There will be more Great Floods.

The Great Flood created new bodies of water such as seas, lakes and rivers. It turned the earth over and rejuvenated it. It rid the earth of the Nephilim giants but a few of them did survive the flood. The Nephilim giants were cannibals who ate human beings. The very tall men ten feet tall or more who were discovered on Easter Island in the 1700's were their descendants.

The Gulf Stream is not a natural phenomenon but it was engineered by many extraterrestrials more than 7,000,000 years ago. The purpose was to keep the lands to what is now Europe warmer.

384,751 years ago a nuclear explosion created the Libyan Desert Glass but it was not caused by people. It was caused by natural gasses.

A large asteroid that hit the earth 91,562,551 years ago caused the extinction of many of the huge animals that threatened the existence of humanity. This event was a natural phenomenon without the influence of extraterrestrials.

A giant meteor hit the earth 8,643,447 years ago and was followed by earthquakes that triggered a climate change that caused the distinction of dinosaurs. It was intentionally directed to Earth by extraterrestrials in part to get rid of the dinosaurs. Dinosaurs have now shrunk down to many little lizards. Lizards and many of the reptiles today were dinosaurs at one time.

When the meteor hit the earth and the dinosaurs were destroyed, some animals survived underground and some of those species are still in existence today: ants, frogs, turtles and little animals.

Since many ancient cities have been discovered beneath the water in the Mediterranean Sea, we can assume the sea was dry land before the Great Flood. It was the Great Flood that covered those cities.

In the ancient past what is now the New York City area was located 40 miles from the ocean. Like everything else a long time ago, it was much further inland and then the ocean rose. The ocean rose and then shrank and then shrank again. This is a process that goes on repeatedly over and over again throughout history.

12,980 years ago a comet hit the earth and caused the coldest deep freeze ice age. The Great Flood and the destruction of Atlantis began when the earth began to warm up at the end of the Ice Age because of the rising sea levels.

Although it was once a land with lush vegetation more than 200, 000 years ago, the cause of the creation of the Sahara Desert was sand storms. It was not an earthquake or a meteorite. It was the wind and the shifting of sand.

There are extensive ruins of ancient civilizations that predate the continent of Atlantis beneath the sands of the Sahara Dessert more than a hundred feet to forty miles beneath the surface. Some of those ruins will be discovered within 100 years.

Noah played a significant role in aiding the evolution of human beings. He was an extraterrestrial who worked with embryos. The ark was a spaceship and the animals were not animals but they were the embryos or the DNA of animals and in that way they were able to put thousands of animals into the spaceship.

There are no physical remains that archeologists will ever find because it never existed as such. Noah in the Bible and humans who lived on Earth before him had physical features somewhat different from ours. He was not the founder of city of Zion which later became the city of Jerusalem

## Remains of ancient civilizations

The prehistoric cave paintings throughout the world can be considered something like a key to our understanding of the history and the future of mankind. There is hidden meaning in those drawings, the interpretation of which tells our history and our future. The drawings in the caves of Lascaux in France are means of communication, writings by both Earth people and extraterrestrials.

The ancient elongated skulls found in Egypt and in the Americas were of alien origin and some were a mixture of aliens and humans. The humans tried to imitate the aliens by forcing the skulls to become longer.

There are many cities that existed before the Great Flood whose remnants remain to this day under water. Lake Titicaca in Peru and its underwater city with sunken ruins were there eons ago. The lake was there before the Great Flood when an earthquake occurred and it was covered with earth and then with water. The existence of the same type of hieroglyphs and cuneiform writings in both the area near Lake Titicaca in Peru and in ancient Sumer and can be explained the same way as in some caverns. They are writings and messages left for the future.

The Lemurians played a role in the creation of the many large statues on Easter Island which represented extraterrestrials and people of stature. They were manmade products of people they worshipped. Extraterrestrials provided the technology for the construction and humans provided the labor because they had more strength. The cause of huge statues on Easter Island to topple over and the population to be greatly diminished was because of the earth moving slowly and toppling them.

The great pyramid at Giza, whose construction began 6,000 years ago, was a power plant to provide electricity before the Great Flood. Extraterrestrials designed the pyramid using their technology and human slaves were forced to do the very difficult work. Pyramids all around the world were built to create energy; not just for use on Earth but also available for use in outer space. The Cheops pyramid in Egypt was built by man power.

The architects of the pyramids in the Yucatan and Guatemala were of another star system; the Pleiades, one of the most advanced groups. They also built the pyramids in Egypt that they could reach from the top down. Humans provided the labor for all the pyramids but extraterrestrials provided the technology.

There is some validity and accuracy in the books called *The Pyramid Power* and *The Pyramid Prophecies* written by Max Toth.

What we call the fallen angels were originally very tall inhabitants of the planet Jupiter who disobeyed orders when they mated with Earth people whose offspring were called the Nephilim giants. There are still physical giants of both male and female gender in Antarctica. There are also giants asleep in various stasis chambers throughout the world. They are from ten feet tall to fifteen feet tall but they don't feel they were giants. They were not angels.

The planetary influence on physical beings determines their height. For example, if they were on Saturn they might have been fifteen feet tall but when they come to Earth, the earth's atmosphere or influence after generations caused them to be much shorter. They will become much shorter and there are adults that are the size of children. They have been recognized already by some intuitives who have seen them. In the Bible we refer to those tall people who were on Earth at one time as the Nephilim. Goliath was one of them.

The original pyramids in Egypt were constructed several thousand years ago and had a covering of white limestone that resembled marble. They were very polished and reflected somewhat like a mirror; much different than they are now. They were beautiful structures and over time the weather worked on them and made them look like they do today.

Hieroglyphs, the early written form of language, were not provided to humans by extraterrestrials.

It was solely for extraterrestrial observation and their travel that the ancient humans placed so much focus on astronomy by building a great number of observatories throughout the world.

The ancient rulers of various lands throughout the world had reptilian bloodlines as some of the ancient stone carvings show.

# ANGELS AND THE DEVIC KINGDOM

Angels are conscious entities whose work is primarily to assist humans and spirits in their evolutionary process. They are gathered everywhere and are always there to help you.

Angels will always remain angels and they do not evolve beyond the angel state but there is potential for humans to eventually evolve to a level parallel yet above that of the angels. Those in the human or spirit realm will never evolve into the angelic kingdom because the two kingdoms are always separate. Humans can evolve to a state that they are like angels but they will not be angels. We refer to them as what is commonly called the "masters".

Everyone has an angel guide that protects them throughout their entire life; some people with two or more. Just as you have a spirit guide who stays with you through your physical life, you also have a specific angel to help and protect you. The angel you have is not related to the month and day you were born; but is assigned to watch over you. It would not be of benefit to know the names of angels because you cannot access them by calling out their names. Angels want to do their activities from behind the scenes.

Even though you may not be consciously aware of your spirit guides or angels, it is good to express your gratitude to them.

Angels sometimes manifest themselves as your pets that remain with you and also as extraterrestrials, bolts of lightning, or anything they wish, including physical human beings. By their appearance, it is not possible to tell the difference between a human and an angel manifesting itself as a human. People often see angels that they believe are humans. It is often the manifestation of an angel when people report that they have seen the Virgin Mary. Like spirits, angels do not have gender but they can portray themselves as whichever gender they choose.

They often manifest themselves to humans as butterflies or dragonflies. When butterflies appear to people after a loved one has died, it is often manifestations of angels or a comforting communication to their loved ones.

Angels have the capability to create things in our world with just their minds, much the same way as spirits do in the spirit world. They can manipulate physical laws when they assist humans, such as the weather, gravity etc. Highly evolved humans also can do the same if they wish to. Events that people consider to be miracles are often the work of angels.

They do not have the ability to change your desires because in doing so they would violate the concept of free will. Angels do not override your free will but they influence it by often projecting thoughts into your head. When you want to do something that will harm yourself or others, angels have the ability to influence your thoughts but not change your desires. They project thoughts to you that are intended to cause you to change your mind. You decide how you react to the thought.

What we call the fallen angels were originally very tall inhabitants of the planet Jupiter who disobeyed orders when they mated with Earth people whose offspring were called the Nephilim giants. The role of the angels described as the Watchers was to pass on knowledge to humans to make them aware. The Incan god Viracocha was one of the angels described as the Watchers in the book of Enoch.

Angels help you when you pray to God to answer your prayers. When you wish to seek help from someone in the spirit world or from the angels it makes no difference whether you just think what you want or whether you say it out loud because they can read your mind. Just think your request and the angels will help. Angels can act immediately.

Homosexuals can become heterosexuals if they ask angels to help them change their orientation. When angels assist, it is not an infringement of the person's free will. If you are having difficulty doing something, angels will sometimes assist you even if you don't ask for assistance. What you refer to as luck can be the result of assistance or protection from the angels or spirits.

The Theosophical concept of the Devic kingdom which includes angels, nature spirits and other types of entities is correct. In addition to working with humans and spirits, angels also work with animals. They do not work with the vegetable kingdom because elementals often referred to as nature spirits, take care of the vegetable kingdom. Elementals include Fairies, Pixies, Elves, Gnomes, Crystal Beings, Stone Beings, Wood Nymphs and Brownies.

They are not on the same line of evolution as angels but they begin at the same point as angels but then take a different path. The various kinds of elementals assist everything that is provided by nature. Each type serves a different purpose. They have free will and, like angels, they always make the correct decisions. It makes elementals want to work harder on their work when they perceive the love a person has for his garden or other facets of nature.

Some elementals appear very childlike and like to play with humans. Some humans can see them. Elementals are not a negative force; but always a positive force. Elementals and angels communicate with each other and with humans through telepathy.

Angels go through the same initial process of evolution as do humans; evolving through the mineral kingdom, the vegetable kingdom and the animal kingdom as do humans. All birds and insects eventually evolve into angels; the same as all animals eventually evolve into humans. Angels do not incarnate although they can show themselves as humans. Butterflies become angels; and angels can also show themselves as butterflies.

Birds and insects are part of the evolutionary path of angels but the type of bird or insect does not determine what type of angel they will become.

There are many different species of angels that serve different roles, one of which is to help humans in their evolution. The extent of the ability of angels depends on what kind of angel they are. Some angels have greater abilities than others. The form that the Seraphim angels often show themselves is similar to serpents with wings. Color exists in the non-physical world and angels actually do radiate colors.

Angels can exercise their free will to assist people without having received instructions from a higher level to do so.

Angels channel information to humans as the spirits do. Angels do not have to verbally communicate.

Extraterrestrials and angels are always two distinct types of entities. In the Bible there were accounts of extraterrestrials whom people believed to be angels.

Angels have free will, but do not have attitudes, emotions and desires such as we have. They do not make wrong decisions in their dealings with people.

The construction, growth and maintenance of bodies of humans are controlled by numerous entities from other realms related to the angelic kingdom.

There is not more overt communication between spirits and angels than there is with humans

Angels were created before the creation of humans. Angels created humans but not the soul.

Jesus was not the incarnation of the Archangel Michael but there is a special bond between them. The angel Gabriel did not dictate the Koran to Mohammad but there were extraterrestrials involved in the writing of the Koran.

There is no specific angel watching over specific countries but all the angels are watching over all the countries.

The pendulum can be used to zero in on whom you have met that is an angel.

# CREATION AND THE UNIVERSE

## The creator

The creator, whom we refer to as God, is a specific entity, more than merely a force. This entity manifests itself in everything that exists, whether it is mineral, vegetable, animal, human, spirit or anything else. There is only one creator god but many lesser gods. The place where God dwells is everywhere. There is no place that God does not dwell. Both good and evil are part of God. What we call evil depends on opinion or point of view. In essence there is no difference between good and evil.

## The universe

There is another planet in our solar system which is eight times further away from the sun than the planet Neptune. That planet has always been in our solar system. It is the planet that the ancient Sumerian stone tablets refer to as Niburu. Niburu has come close to Earth many times in the past and always causes major Earth changes when it does. It will cause what we consider harm to humanity when it comes near Earth.

Niburu has moons revolving around it. It revolves around our entire solar system and takes a little more than 5000 years to revolve around it. The moons around Niburu are inhabited by human extraterrestrials that are more advanced than Earth humans. They are of a kind, friendly nature and they are humans that appear like us. They will make contact with Earth humans and the relationship will be friendly.

When Zachariah Sitchin interpreted the Sumerian tablets that described Niburu, he was channeling his higher self but was discredited by scientists because he did not have the proper credentials to make such proclamations. He was a highly evolved soul. Likewise the information in this book will also not be credible to most people because the channeler did not have the proper credentials.

There are additional undiscovered planets in our solar system, nine as large as the earth. They are as far away as the planet Niburu. Pluto was originally a moon of Saturn that was hit by the planet Niburu. Niburu influenced it and threw it out of the orbit of Saturn.

An ancient Sumerian tablet said that there was once a planet between Jupiter and Mars that they called Tiamat. That planet created both the asteroid belt and the planet Earth. The earth was once part of Tiamat. The destruction of the planet Tiamat was not the result of warring extraterrestrial groups. Some of the survivors of that planet went to the dwarf planet Ceres and some went to Earth. Ceres was not a moon of another planet.

The creation, placement and purpose of the dwarf planet Ceres inside the orbit of Neptune followed the same pattern as that of our moon. There are human inhabitants who live in the interior of Ceres that look just like Earth humans. Their thinking is different from that of Earth people. If you were to meet them, you would not like them; in part because of the difference of lifestyles. They are not as warlike as the people of Earth. No one from Ceres has come to Earth and no one from Earth has gone to Ceres. We will come in contact with them on a widespread basis about 9100 years from now.

Earth was inhabited by spirits before it was inhabited by humans. It is the most recent planet to be inhabited by human entities. Human life on Earth is the least advanced of all planets. Physical life on

Earth is more difficult than that physical life in any other place in the universe to live because its inhabitants make it so. There are more rules and regulations on Earth than there are on other planets. The people on other planets are nicer to each other than Earth people are to one other. There is no other planet on which humans are at the same level of evolution as Earth humans.

It was because of Lucifer's actions that the earth became the most difficult place for physical life. Lucifer has definite intentions and they are misguided. His intentions in regard to the involvement with Earth are good but we don't view them as such.

There was a time that Mars resembled Earth in regard to land features, vegetation and animal life as well as human life. Mars was once like Earth with water, land features, vegetation and atmosphere.

The rings around Saturn were originally a band around the planet built by humans to be a super weapon that could destroy other planets. It was designed to be a very powerful weapon used for protection. The band was destroyed by warring extraterrestrials when it broke up to become the rings.

There are technological ruins from ancient civilizations, such as objects comparable to our computers, in the rings of the planet Saturn. At one time there was a flourishing highly advanced civilization there that has been long gone.

Just as the outward universe with all the celestial bodies is infinite and forever expanding, the inward universe inside the atom is also infinite and expanding. There are whole universes inside the atom. Some advanced Earth people can see inside the atom. There are untold numbers of universes; as many below as above. Splitting the atom does not cause damage to universes.

Below is very important, not just on the earth but beneath the earth. There is activity going on beneath the earth and in the oceans, not just on the surface of the earth.

There are pyramids on the moon and on Mars and on other planets in our solar system. There are also pyramids outside of our solar system. There are pyramids beneath the water on our planet because the level of water has risen and the earth has fallen.

There are humans on other planets and moons throughout the universe and in our solar system on/in which there are humans who appear exactly like us. There are hundreds of millions of planets within the Milky Way which could support human life as we now are.

Just as there are many different physical worlds, there are also many different spirit worlds. There are multiple spirit worlds just as there are multiple physical worlds. Each planet or moon that has human life has a spirit world. All spirit worlds are not alike. The character of a spirit world depends on the planet it is part of. Spirit worlds exist on planets and other celestial bodies where no physical human life exists.

Millions of humans who appear just like us live in a highly evolved civilization beneath the ice in Antarctica. There are entire cities that are inhabited by extraterrestrials. Air and water are necessary for the entities beneath the surface of Antarctica. They are necessary for flowers and anything that needs air or water. There is also vegetable and animal life beneath the surface. They are somewhat different from what is on the surface of the earth. The Nazis were involved with the civilization in Antarctica. They are still there but not as actively involved as they once were.

There are twenty-four moons in our solar system inside of which human extraterrestrials live. Each of these moons has a spirit world component.

There are no stars at the very center of our constellation, the Milky Way, because there is a very powerful force there. It is what scientists call a black hole. A black hole sucks anything into it that is less than 100 light years away. It is because of that energy that there are no stars present. A black hole is anti-matter. Matter and anti-matter are two sides of the same coin. The coin is the universe.

Human life does not exist on the surface of moons or planets that are far from the sun. It exists inside the moons of planets rather than inside the planet itself.

The first humans that appear on a planet are transplants from another planet. Extraterrestrials go there to seed the planet with humans. Human life and animal life do not appear on a planet at approximately the same time.

That is different from the way Earth was populated by humans. Earth humans were developed as the creations of the Anunnaki extraterrestrials. Over millions of years the Anunnaki injected some of their own DNA into a bi-ped animal that was already on Earth before their arrival. Little by little Earth humans are becoming increasingly like the Anunnaki. The process of injecting DNA is continuing today and will continue for millions of years.

There is more than one star in our solar system. The earth revolves around more than just what we think of as our sun.

There are spirits everywhere in the universe even though physical beings are not everywhere. They can instantaneously travel from one spirit world to another.

There is less animal life in the sea than there is on land on Earth. There is also less vegetation in the sea than on land.

Throughout the universe there is a spirit world connected to every celestial body where humans reside. Most inhabitants of a celestial body usually reincarnate on or inside the same celestial body each time they re-enter the physical world. There are planets on which there is animal life but no humans.

## The moon

Our moon is both a technological artifact and a natural formation. It is a natural creation that was greatly modified by extraterrestrials. It was originally somewhere else, but by using their technology, they moved it to a specific place so that life on Earth could take place exactly as it now is. Our moon is hollow inside and has a metallic covering on top of which is about three feet of something similar to dust. When astronauts crashed something on the moon, it rang like a bell for about an hour, showing that it was hollow inside. The moon serves as a space station and there are extraterrestrials living inside of it. Our moon was not originally a satellite of the planet Tiamat.

The major purpose for which the moon was created and placed where it is 784,741 years ago was to enable life on Earth to be as it currently is.

Extraterrestrials currently inhabit the interior of the moon because the actions of Earth people can be observed more easily from there than from elsewhere. By being there they can prevent certain kinds of activities from taking place. One of those activities is atomic warfare.

The side of the moon not facing the earth is different from what we see. Spaceships often land there and take off from there. UFO's that come to Earth from other places in the universe always go to the moon first. The moon serves as a landing port for UFO's that come to Earth

Extraterrestrials inside the moon look just like Earth humans. Many of them spend their entire lifetime inside the moon. Their lifetimes are often approximately 1500 years. When they reincarnate they sometimes come back to the moon but they usually reincarnate elsewhere.

The earth was inhabited by animal life before the placement of the moon. There was biped animal life but no human life before the placement of the moon.

Although all physical life on the moon is beneath the surface, there is spirit life in the atmosphere.

## Stargates

Places exist in our planet where people can go through a portal and emerge in faraway places in the universe and also go into the future and into the past. We refer to them as stargates or wormholes. They are located both on land and in water. There is a network of underwater portals on Earth used by extraterrestrials. There is a black hole in our galaxy that has a white hole at the other end of it but this is not a stargate that aliens travel through.

There are thirteen stargates in the United States, including the Bermuda Triangle and the Michigan Triangle. There are also stargates in area 51 in Nevada, in California and in Massachusetts. There are 280 stargates in the world, including some in Antarctica where UFO's, can go below the ice where there are extraterrestrial developments.

Saddam Husain discovered a stargate as did Hitler.

The Russians, Chinese, Japanese, Europeans, South Americans and people from twenty-two countries on all continents use stargates.

There are people living in the United States who go through stargates to work off planet on the moon, Mars and other moons and planets in our solar systems but none outside of our solar system.

# DEATH

Dying is as easy as falling asleep and then waking up in a different place. Although the death process is not painful, most humans have a great fear of dying. In reality the only basis for that fear is the unknown. The transition from the physical world to the spirit world is not necessarily easier if you are knowledgeable about the spirit world before you die.

The length of peoples' lives is predestined before incarnation but it can be shortened by their actions or when there are catastrophic events such as war, typhoons, mass murders in which hundreds of people are killed. All of those people were not destined to die at that time. The length is sometimes, but rarely, lengthened by the person's actions and even by the actions of others.

When you die and discard your physical bodies, you do not retain the same attitudes, emotions, and desires when you cross over to the world of spirits. If you are angry when you die, you will take over that same emotion for only the moment. The attitudes, emotions, and desires that you have in the physical dissipate over time after you enter the spirit world.

Those that are based on physical appetites such as food, alcohol, drugs and sex cannot be satisfied in the spirit world. This is not one of the concepts of hell but it is torture. There are times that people who have mental or emotional disorders carry over those same disorders when they arrive in the spirit world. They can overcome the disorders in the spirit world before they reincarnate.

At the moment of death, a review of your whole lifetime flashes before you and everything you have done then comes to your memory but that memory does not stay with you. After you cross over to the spirit world, you will be able to recall all the events of your recent lifetime with clarity if you so choose and you can even recall events that you could not recall while in the physical. You are not forced to be confronted with all the memories of your recent lifetime if you do not want to relive those memories.

After a person dies, there is no need to wait before any actions are taken that might shock the departed soul to realize that have died. However, some religions say to cover the tombstone for a while. This is because they believe that recently departed people do not always know they are dead for a while after they have crossed over.

Your spirit guide is there to meet you just when you enter the spirit world and people who love you will also be there to assist and bring you comfort. Family members and friends are able to help with the transition when they greet you upon your arrival. Your pets can be there also. Angels are not involved in helping people cross over.

There is no such thing as religion in the spirit world and God didn't create any religions. Most people lose their religious beliefs when they enter the spirit world. Terrorists who have killed in the name of their religion still have the same attitudes but they don't have their religious beliefs. Those who have committed an atrocious crime, such as mass murderer suicide bombers, feel they were justified in doing and continue to feel justified for what they did after they have crossed over into the spirit world.

When they enter the spirit world, people who were very religious often have difficulty in accepting the fact that religion is manmade and does not exist in the spirit world but those in the spirit world eventually get over the idea of religion.

There is a place that is neither the physical world nor the spirit world that we refer to as the in-between earthbound world. Nineteen percent of people go to that world for a while after they die. They stay earthbound for varying amounts of time. People do not have to enter the spirit world immediately after they die or as you say "follow the light".

Spirits can become earthbound if they do not follow the light and go into the spirit world. By telling departed people to follow the light, it is possible for humans to help them make the transition to the spirit world and spirits can also help them. If you have very strong attachments to your earthly possessions when you die, you can be attracted to stay in the in-between physical world.

There are many, many earthbound spirits who are confused and are not fully in the spirit world. Sometimes those that are alive keep spirits earthbound by excessively mourning them or by keeping their personal possessions too long. You do not hold back those who have passed on when you think happy memories of them.

Strong willed people can take measures while they are alive that would assure that they do not become earthbound when they die. If you die and want to go directly into the spirit world and not be in the in-between world, you can prevent yourself from being earthbound by thinking the right thoughts.

People sometimes continue to feel physical pain for a while after they die because pain is felt in what some refer to as the etheric body. The etheric body connects the physical body and the spirit body by a silver cord. When the cord is severed, death occurs. Pain occurs when the etheric body has not fully separated from the spirit body. The same is true when a person feels pain in a leg or arm that has been amputated. The etheric body is never needed after death.

There is sometimes a danger if a person is cremated too soon after dying because the etheric body may not have fully separated from the physical body, thus causing the entity to feel pain. For that reason you should not be cremated right away but you should wait two or three days. When a person is cremated, the soul evolves no differently than if the person were buried in the ground. Cremation absolutely does not hurt the soul.

When fetuses die in the womb, it has been predestined; the same as when very young children die. The means by which you die is predestined in the spirit world before reincarnation. This could include by heart attack, drowning, being murdered, or even by suicide. The means of death do not always happen that way because the exercise of a person's will and subsequent actions can alter predestiny.

The average lifespan of humans 100 years from now will be 89 years. The average lifespan of earth humans is shorter than those on other planets; both those who look like humans and those who don't. Some can live more than 30,000 years.

When you pass over, it is not important to have a funeral with a priest or rabbi or minister to assure the safe passing. Even though having a funeral or a memorial service does not help you to get on the other side more comfortably, it does help the people that are going to the funeral.

There are sometimes occasions when at least part of a person's consciousness remains for a while at the gravesite. The part that remains earthbound is what we call a "ghost" as contrasted with a "spirit", the part that moves to the spirit world.

There is no one factor that is more prevalent than others in determining how easily you will adjust to the transition to the spirit world. The transition to the spirit world or your life in the spirit world would be more difficult if you were hated by many people because of your evil deeds while in the physical.

People who hoard many physical objects because they are emotionally unable to dispose of them have difficulty adjusting to the transition to the spirit world and are likely to become earthbound.

People who are very materialistic and emotionally attached to their possessions have more difficulty adjusting to life in the spirit world than people who are not materialistic.

People who are in a state of mind where they expect to die soon or consciously want to die make their transition to the spirit world easier. The same is true when a person has no fear of dying. However, it is not necessarily easier to adjust to life in the spirit world after making the transition.

A person's level of intelligence carries over from the physical world to the spirit world. The level of intelligence is not necessarily carried over with the transition back to the physical world from the spirit world.

Some people know exactly what they were doing when they died. When souls cross over to the spirit world, some need long periods of rest while others need very little or practically none at all.

When they pass over into the spirit world while in a coma or are heavily drugged with medication, some people are immediately alert and some are not.

The transition from the physical world to the spirit will be easier for people who are interested in helping other people rather than those who have been selfishly materialistic.

After a person dies it can be emotionally difficult for the spirit when humans say critical or harmful things about him that they never said while he was in the physical.

Elizabeth Kubler Ross was correct when she said that when a person's death is imminent, friends and relatives should not encourage that person to hold onto life but should give them permission to die.

When death is imminent, people sometimes wait for certain conditions to be right before they die; conditions such as loved relatives or friends being present at the time of departure.

Your decision about when to go is made at the soul level. You are aware of it at the subconscious level but not at the conscious level.

The transition to the spirit world is not any different for those who have Alzheimer's disease than it is for others.

Humans who are able to see auras emanating around the physical bodies of people can no longer see their auras before they die.

There are many levels in the spirit world and when you cross over to that world, you reside at the level which matches your actions when you were in this world.

When people have what we refer to as a near death experience, some enter the spirit world and some do not. Near death experiences are spontaneous and cannot be preplanned.

Although many religions teach you that when you die you go immediately to either heaven or to hell there are no such places but they are states of mind.

A person's age at the time of passing into the spirit world has no effect on his transition to the spirit world or his life in the spirit world.

Spoken language isn't necessary when you cross over because spirits can read minds.

At the soul level, sometimes a spouse chooses to die in order to allow the other to go in a different direction.

Sometimes spirits are able to communicate to mediums immediately after they cross over but then must spend a long period of no communication before they begin communicating again.

When people cross over to the spirit world, they are able to see themselves more accurately than they did when they were alive.

When someone passes over, they cannot leave their energies on a person so the person who is still alive acts just like them.

Disposing of a person's possessions very soon after they die could have an emotional effect for a while on that person as a spirit.

# EVENTS OF THE COMMON ERA

## Prior to the 18th century

When the Romans destroyed the ancient library at Alexandria Egypt, great numbers of the manuscripts were saved and taken to Rome and kept in the Vatican

Machu Picchu in Peru was abandoned after a hundred or so years because it was not very comfortable to live there. It was very high in altitude. The climate and its past history had a tendency to have some reflection on those that are fearful of living there. Most of the people didn't survive because of the climate.

The Mayan Indians had settlements everywhere, not just in Mexico but also in many places in what is now the United States. Approximately ninety-five percent of the Mayan civilization disappeared more than 1000 years ago, long before the arrival of the Europeans because of earthquakes. There were earthquakes in Central America where the Mayans lived.

The Incan empire was created and influenced by extraterrestrials.

There was assistance from extraterrestrials in the creation of the maps copied by Piri Reis about five centuries ago because when they stand on a higher hill, they see more of the mountain.

The magician Merlin as portrayed in the Arthurian legends of England did not exist. It is made up stories concocted by people.

The letter about Jesus supposedly written by Pontius Pilate to the Emperor Tiberius was a forgery written several centuries later.

Christopher Columbus was in search of a passage to the East but he was not interested in finding Atlantis. What he saw rising from the sea was not a UFO but it was a natural phenomenon.

The Black Plague was intentionally designed by extraterrestrials for rats to reduce the earth's population. At the present we also are working on decreasing the world's population by both physical disease and warfare.

Leonardo DaVinci's painting of the Mona Lisa is, in a way, a self portrait. It's the feminine part of him that he's expressing. It is not a painting of an actual person. It is more or less a self-portrait he created with his smile.

Freemasonry was encoded in the design of Shakespeare's Globe Theater. The number 72 plays a significant role in its design. The number 72 is 9 and if you put it upside down it is evil. The design of the theater incorporates secret hermetic knowledge.

Centuries ago the Indians threw a great amount gold into the lakes in South America so the Spaniards could not take possession of it. There is still a lot of gold at the bottom of many of the lakes in South America.

The huge underground city which could house 20,000 people in Derinkuyu in Turkey was built by slaves not by extraterrestrials. It was built to be a safe place. Humans built the city without advice from extraterrestrials.

There is historical basis for the existence of the city that we refer to as El Dorado. Lake Guatavita in Colombia has nothing to do with El Dorado.

The cause of the disappearance of the lost colony of Roanoke, Virginia in 1587 was a huge sink hole. The earth swallowed them. It wasn't unfriendly Indians.

Joan of Arc was influenced by extraterrestrials in order to avoid the negative consequences if the English won the battle against the French.

About 400 people danced uncontrollably for many hours and days, some until they became very ill or even died, in Strasbourg, France in 1518. The cause was a certain plant beneath their feet. It was a hallucinogenic drug, not marihuana but some other kind of plant.

In the Christian Bible, there is a description of an event which took place in what they called an upper room and suddenly everyone started speaking in Tongues, the language that extraterrestrials speak. They were channeling extraterrestrials.

The Byzantine emperor Constantine IV in the $7^{th}$ century AD defeated the invaders by destroying more than one thousand ships with something called Greek fire. This was fire that could not be extinguished with water. Its formula was later lost and never rediscovered. Greek fire that would burn under water was actually oil.

Several centuries ago some French noblemen called the Knights Templar went to Jerusalem in search of King Solomon's treasure and brought treasures of great wealth back to France. The Knights Templar became the forerunners of the Freemasons. The Freemasons had a profound effect of the creation of our country.

They were part of the Illuminati but since then the Illuminati have changed to become a negative. The Freemasons pirated pirate ships to plunder gold from the ocean vessels of the various countries. That gold was to enrich the Illuminati.

Sir Francis Bacon was the illegitimate son of Queen Elizabeth I of England. He actually wrote most of the works that Shakespeare dictated to him because Shakespeare didn't know how to write. Bacon could be considered as the father of Freemasonry.

The Freemasons had a significant impact on the founding of our country. The source of the Freemasons' information was extraterrestrial.

The Priory of Sion a hoax but there is some truth in it. It promotes the marriage of Jesus to Mary Magdalene and their descendents to prove a secret bloodline of the Merovingian Dynasty on the thrones of France and the rest of Europe. It proves that the kings of France are the descendants of Jesus.

## The 18th and 19th centuries

The purpose of the street designs in Washington D.C. was that they could be seen from any angle. The design of the city was a plan based on ancient wisdom.

It was not an experiment in democracy but rather a learning point that extraterrestrials were involved in the founding of our country. It was for the purpose of establishing a new pattern for government for other countries. Some of the major founding fathers of this country were influenced by both higher level spirits and extraterrestrials.

Although some people believe that there was extraterrestrial or angel involvement in aiding the Americans in the fight against the British in the War of 1812 in regard to the manipulation of weather conditions, that is not true.

Napoleon Bonaparte and Adolf Hitler were antichrists that Nostradamus predicted. Throughout history there were, are and will be many antichrists. Currently there are 2898 antichrists on Earth.

Abraham Lincoln was psychic and he received guidance from the spirit world through a medium. He wrote the Emancipation Proclamation himself. He was an intelligent man who meant only well. He believed in extraterrestrials as did his wife. He knew his life's plan and that he would die young through assassination but he didn't believe it. He has not reincarnated because his work in the spirit world is keeping him from reincarnating.

The assassination of President Lincoln was the work of John Wilkes Booth but there were also other people involved. Booth held the gun himself. The assassination of Lincoln was a conspiracy and Andrew Johnson was part of the conspiracy.

Although it has been traditionally believed that the inventor of the telephone was Alexander Graham Bell, the inventor was actually Elisha Gray but Bell had more publicity.

In 1892 Lizzie Borden murdered her father and stepmother with an axe because she was both demented and very angry. She was treated badly and avenging them.

The American Revolution became an anti-Illuminati revolt.

## The 20th century

It is interesting that Vice-President Andrew Johnson was involved

in the assassination of President Lincoln and that the person involved with the assassination of President Kennedy was Vice-President Lyndon Johnson. It was just a coincidence that both vice-presidents were named Johnson.

There is a media cover-up regarding the death of John Kennedy. President Johnson was the one who was really involved with the assassination. He disliked Mr. Kennedy and he was jealous of him. He himself wanted to be president. He wanted Kennedy out. He was working in conjunction with the Illuminati. President Johnson knew the assassination was going to occur. He allowed it to happen but was not directly involved.

President Kennedy was predestined to be assassinated and President Johnson was playing a predetermined role. He was also indirectly involved with the assassination of Robert Kennedy. There was no foreign country involved in the assassination of President Kennedy. Robert Kennedy was assassinated as a convenience, just to get him out of the way.

The Kennedy family was one of the thirteen families that were part of the Illuminati. President John Kennedy betrayed the Illuminati by going against what they wanted and was assassinated because of the betrayal. The same is true of Robert Kennedy.

Lee Harvey Oswald was recruited by a government official in the assassination of John Kennedy. He was not involved in recruiting

Jack Ruby. Ruby was honest, faithful and loyal but stupid.

Amelia Earhart's plane crash provided food for cannibals in the jungle in that era. It did not crash in the ocean. It crashed because the oil in the machinery became dry and did not work well.

Princess Diana was accidently killed in the car. It was the fault of the driver who was speeding and under the influence of legal medication and not enough sleep.

The death of the actress Natalie Wood many years ago was accidental when she slipped and fell and drowned, not able to swim.

In 1949 Secretary of Defense Admiral Forrestal was murdered by the government because he had secret knowledge regarding Antarctica. He was not the only person to have this knowledge.

In the 1940's, Admiral Byrd discovered advanced underground civilizations with people living underground at the South Pole. There was a cover-up by our government regarding his expedition to Antarctica after World War II.

The five airplanes that disappeared in the Bermuda Triangle in 1945 went into a stargate and arrived somewhere else in the universe.

Princess Grace Kelly of Monaco was killed in an automobile which her daughter was driving. She was arguing with her mother and she was a young driver of the age of fourteen. It was an accident and it was hush-hushed that the daughter was driving. There was a rumor that the cause of the accident was that Grace Kelly had a stroke but the stroke was after the accident.

The murderer of the Jean Benet Ramsey was a lowly old man who had been imprisoned. He crawled through a basement window of their home and then went into the room of the child and got into bed with her because she appeared as a young adult.

President Eisenhower and some of his advisors had face-to-face discussions with an extraterrestrial named Valiant Thor who said he was from Venus and who looked like a human, in Washington D.C. during the late 1950's. The man actually was a human who lived beneath the surface of Venus.

O.J. Simpson murdered Nicole Brown and Ron Goldman. He had no accomplices. He himself committed the murder. He was under the influence of drugs during the time of the murder. He did not confess to anyone what he did, not even to himself. At the present time he wants to kill another person. He is a very angry, hostile person who is a fuse waiting to be ignited.

Tesla developed what was called a death ray. The use of the death ray caused of a huge explosion in Tunguska Siberia in 1908 that was more than 1000 times more powerful than an atom bomb.

The Russian monk Rasputin was influenced by extraterrestrials and he was also simply deranged.

Although there is speculation that Hitler escaped from Germany and died somewhere else, he died in Germany. He did not die a natural death but was murdered.

In the 1950's the CIA secretly injected LSD into the food supply in a town in France, thus producing severe hallucinations and many deaths

In regard to what happened to Michael Rockefeller in 1961 when his boat apparently overturned of the coast of New Guinea, he was eaten by scavengers. It was a horrible death.

The crash of the airplane in which John Kennedy Jr. was killed was an accident. It was not sabotage. He was blinded by the water. It was pilot error rather than mechanical failure and he was not a very good pilot. He was only thinking of himself. He was in an emotional state at that time with his wife.

Although there Is a rumor that John Kennedy Jr. was not killed in the plane crash but is still alive, that rumor is not true.

In 1947 President Truman established a committee called the Majestic 12 to investigate extraterrestrial activities in the United States. The findings of that committee were very accurate. If we were to read that report we could assume that it is true.

Frederick Valentich and his plane disappeared while flying over water in Australia in 1978. They were abducted by a UFO and went into a stargate.

Dorothy Kilgallen was correct when she wrote newspaper articles about a crashed UFO in England in the 1950's. A UFO actually crashed there.

The bandleader Glen Miller's airplane that crashed in 1944 was ambushed. The plane has disintegrated and will never be located.

James Hoffa, the Teamsters Union leader, disappeared without a trace in 1971 because he was intentionally put into a tank that pulverized him. He was made to disappear so that his body couldn't be identified at all.

Mahatma Gandhi was visited by extraterrestrials that guided him and influenced his thinking.

In the 1980's, President Reagan had face-to-face interaction with extraterrestrials. There was an assassination attempt on him to prevent him from revealing information about extraterrestrials.

President Obama was born in the Hawaii and therefore a naturally born United States citizen.

Although it is rumored that Jimmy Carter was the half-brother of John Kennedy because they have very similar facial features, they were not related. Jimmy Carter is not working with the Alliance in opposition to the Cabal.

The Clintons ran a cocaine business in Arkansas in the 1980's and 1990's. It was clandestine and related to the Iran Contra deal. It helped Iran quite a bit. The Clintons gave financial, industrial and military information to China for which they profited financially. This was done before Clinton became president. Clinton and his wife have been successful in adding money to their own pockets. She is not well mentally and physically. She will not try for another nomination to be president but she will attempt to influence from behind the scenes.

Vince Foster, who worked for the Clintons, committed suicide because he was going to testify against the Clintons and the pressure was too great.

The Cabal was responsible for intentionally establishing the foundation for World War I and World War II to begin so that they could have greater control over the world. We could substitute the word Luciferians for Cabal.

The National Security Agency has designed bitcoins as a backup plan as a currency that cannot be tampered with and which will inhibit monetary control or corruption. The bitcoin is a positive thing. It will come into existence.

In World War II the Japanese captured a great deal of gold from the Southeast Asian countries. That gold is buried in huge bunkers in Vietnam. That is the actual reason our country went to war with North Vietnam. Since that time, the United States government has removed all the gold from Fort Knox and has placed it there. The Cabal controls the gold.

The bombing of the Oklahoma City federal building by Timothy McVey in 1995 was a test run for the destruction of the Wall Street Towers. His bomb was definitely too small to create such a large explosion. It was a controlled demolition by the Cabal. The explosion was orchestrated because all the documents for the Whitewater investigation were in that building. That was exactly what they were trying to destroy. The Clintons are very devious and we will find that out in the future.

In the 1980's the United States and the Soviet Union secretly worked together on establishing a space program and extraterrestrial research. The United States is continuing research that we don't know about.

In the 1940's the actress Heddy Lamar made inventions that made possible today's technology of Wi-Fi, GPS, Bluetooth and even the internet. She was a very amazing lady.

The Nazis developed UFO's in the 1930's. They established colonies or bases on Mars and are still there. They flew over the United States Capitol in 1952 when Eisenhower was president. Since the 1960's they have recruited thousands of highly intelligent people to live on Mars.

President Reagan was aware that the Iran Contra scandal money was used to buy arms for cocaine dealers. At the time he had some information but it wasn't expressed.

Marilyn Monroe died of an overdose of medication. She herself caused her death. It was not someone else. The Kennedy family could not wait to get rid of her but they did not murder her.

During the Franco dictatorship in Spain, thousands of babies were stolen because their parents were opposed to him. Those babies were sold to other parents who supported him.

The United States government intelligence forces informed us in advance that Japan would attack Pearl Harbor and declare war on this country.

**The 21st century**

There a government cover-up regarding the destruction of the World Trade Center Towers. When the airplanes hit Building One and Building Two in the World Trade Center, Building Seven did not collapse in the same manner. The collapse was because of poor structure, not explosives, the mismanagement of electrical wiring.

The present groups of Islamic terrorists are reincarnations of the Nazis and are also the reincarnations of many groups throughout the history of our world. They travel as a group through their incarnations again and again. The Islamic Terrorists have appeared at various times throughout history under different names.

The spread of Lyme's disease was the result of experiments done with ticks by our government on Plum Island, N.Y. The experiments taking place on Plum Island are dangerous for people. Other diseases have also been created by our government's experiments. Most of the hospitals on the North Shore of Long Island have many cancer patients. Experiments are why there has been so much cancer on Long Island.

The ten stones or commandments known as the Guide Stones in Georgia contain coded messages for the impending apocalypse. The thinking of the creator was influenced by the Illuminati.

Saddam Hussein discovered a stargate which he was planning on using for nefarious purposes. He was interested in control, a very controlling person. The United States invaded Iraq because they were aware that he had discovered a stargate. They went after him so he couldn't make use of that stargate. Saddam Hussein thought he was the reincarnation of King Nebuchadnezzar II but he was not. He was insane.

U.S. technology now has an unmanned space shuttle that has been in orbit for two years and is capable of disabling enemy satellites. Disabling satellites has already been done. Israel made the satellite and they know how to use it effectively. The unmanned satellite caused North Korea's satellites to misfire. We are protecting ourselves through that satellite.

Cuba's economy will be restored to a level of prosperity and the lifestyle of its citizens will be greatly elevated when the Castro regime ends with the departure of Raoul Castro. The government will become less socialized and more democratic.

Nikolas Cruz, the mass murderer of high school students, said that for years he was tortured by demon voices in his head that told him to kill. It is true that he heard such voices because he was deranged.

Both President Obama and President Trump were taken to see the civilization under the ice in Antarctica. In a way, the presidents were threatened with extinction if they exposed this. Donald Trump's established a Space Force because he has information about extraterrestrials there that the public does not know.

The main reasons that Supreme Court Justice Kavanaugh was so violently opposed by the Democrats were that he opposed abortion and that he was in favor of military tribunals for civilians accused of treason.

Politicians in our government profited financially from the sale of uranium to Russia in 2010, especially the Clintons. Money will be obsolete someday. The concept of bitcoins or something similar to them will be replacing money.

John McCain's career was not built on lies and deception as some people say. He did not broadcast anti-American propaganda to the Vietnamese people over the radio. He was a very loyal and kind man. John McCain was actually murdered by poison.

Anthony Scalia's death was not self-inflicted. He did not choose to go. He was murdered by opposing Democrat members in the House of Representatives because of his stance on issues they opposed.

In 2011 hundreds of thousands of dead birds and fish were found ashore in Alaska. The deaths were caused by sound waves generated into the air by our HAARP facility that was built to defend underground facilities.

There is a ridiculous theory that no one in the planes that crashed into the Wall Street Towers in 2001 was killed and the passengers were secretly taken off that plane and taken safely to an underground facility where they are secretly living today. The crash purported to have been orchestrated by our government and the plane was remotely controlled.

However, our government was involved in the airplanes that crashed into the Wall Street towers in 2001. It is covering up their involvement with the Wall Street Towers crash. Nuclear weapons that emitted very little radiation were used to destroy the Wall Street Towers in 2001. Some of the first responders died of radiation. Although it was rumored that the Bush family was involved in the destruction of the towers, that is not true.

The cause of Robin William's suicide was by an enemy whom he believed to be a friend.

It is true regarding John of God in Brazil, that more than 600 women came forward and accused him of raping them. A person can actually do what we call miracles such as healing a person from disease and yet perform evil acts.

# EVENTS OF THE PRESENT AND NEAR FUTURE

**As you read this section and some other sections of the book, please keep in mind that the future cannot be predicted with 100 percent accuracy when it involves the exercise of a person's free will. If it could be predicted with 100 percent accuracy, then the will would not be free. Instead, predictions are based on how people's decisions were made in similar past situations. It is also possible that some events will have occurred before the publication of this book.**

## The media

The media in the United States are as controlled, dishonest or biased as some people portray them to be. Everything is a secret. The media are not honest and actually do provide fake news. The press is one-sided and tells us mostly just one side. The five major media companies are somewhat controlled by the Cabal. Even the Fox news channel is controlled by the Cabal. They cannot be trusted the way we would like to trust them. No news source can be trusted. Social media programs are manipulated by their creators to be of assistance to the Deep State. It is all manipulated. There are currently CIA operatives in the media. It has always been that way.

## The Cabal and the Alliance

Our society is divided into two opposing groups which are the descendants of two ancient warring extraterrestrial civilizations.

The opposition to each other can be noted in the current political situations throughout the world.

They are currently referred to as the Alliance and the Cabal. There are members of both the Cabal and the Alliance in both the Republican Party and the Democrat Party. There are not more members of the Cabal in either party. Both parties are equally mixed with members of the Cabal.

The Cabal is an umbrella term which includes the Illuminati, the deep state and the One World Order and other dark forces which should be eliminated. Our government is very deceitful to us and they do not tell us all that is true. There are both Republican and Democrat elected government officials who are instruments of the Cabal. It is not just one party. It is both parties. Both are to blame but one will be eliminated. The one that will be eliminated is dominated by the Cabal.

The Cabal is working toward the dumbing down of America. They are brainwashing people and practicing mind control through popular music and other forms of media entertainment such as the super bowl commercials, the Grammy Awards and ballgames. The simplest people will be ignited by the Cabal.

## Popular culture

Many of the current popular music artists are instruments of the Cabal as are the media. The same is true of movie and TV stars. The media are very much controlled by the Cabal. We have something to fear from the Cabal. The lyrics of pop music perpetuate American idiocracy. The IQ level of the lyrics has dropped dramatically within the past generation. The mentality of those with us has been very short limited.

There are forces that are part of the dumbing down of America and the lyrics are part of that. The reason for that is so they can get control of people. They are doing a good job. The same is true of the movies that come out. Television programs are dumbing down people too. Hip-hop music was created or used to promote criminal behavior. You Tube is used by the Deep State to lead people into their way of thinking and belief system. The same is true of Google.

The Cabal is very much engaged in our government. For many years they have been here to disrupt and will continue to disrupt and be that way. Our government is controlled by the Cabal but the people in the country are not as controlled as much as the government is. There seems to be a war underneath it all but no war will come from it.

The information that Edward Snowden provides about the Cabal is aiding in their downfall and other factions of the Cabal. He wants to discourage the Cabal. He has a great deal more information that could shake our political scene. He has secret information about the activities of extraterrestrials on Earth. The government is hiding this information because they do not want to cause any fear and also because they want control.

The Euro is a creation of the Cabal. It would assist them to have control over humanity.

General Flynn was unjustly targeted by the Mueller investigation because he has much information that the Deep State does not want disclosed. There is corruption or influence from the Cabal on the United States Supreme Court.

## Forces influencing our politics

There has always been voter fraud. We should go back to counting of the ballots. Much voter fraud could be eliminated if more people were to use paper ballots instead of the use of the computer. George Soros owns much of the software that is used to tabulate computer voting. He is manipulating those results. He is trying to control the outcome of elections by creating voter fraud. The company that makes computers is not involved. Everyone has some influence. Our government is not becoming increasingly corrupt because it has always been corrupt and it always will be corrupt.

Other countries are covertly influencing American politics at this time. One of those countries is Russia. Americans are very confused and not together. They should join each other. Extraterrestrials are influencing American politics. Different extraterrestrials are influencing one party and other groups are influencing the other party. Our political arena is a contest between different extraterrestrials groups.

There was some voter fraud in the 2016 presidential election, but not much. It was mostly under control but more prevalent in California than elsewhere. The person that won was supposed to win.

There was a spy, or whatever we want to call it, placed in the Trump campaign but President Obama was not knowledgeable about it.

Many of the large corporations in our country have negative intents regarding the direction or future of our country.

The promoting of political correctness is an attempt to stifle free speech to the point that people can be controlled.

There are factions in our government that have amassed a great deal of information about thousands of people in our country, information that they will use as a form of blackmail to keep them in line.

## Political, social and economic unrest

It is sometimes true that the current social unrest and humans disregard for other humans is related to the effect of planetary alignments but it is not related to the approaching of the planet Niburu. The origin of our current political unrest dates back to much earlier than the time of Atlantis.

The agenda of the Republican Party is influenced more by the Alliance and the Democrats are influenced more by the Cabal.

There will be increasing civil unrest in our country. Many lives will be lost because of that. It is occurring at this moment. Civil unrest will become so bad that martial law will have to be imposed in some parts of the country. That will not be as bad as it was during the time of our Civil War. Many people will be killed. The unrest is those who are privileged and those who are not; those who have money and those who do not.

Within the next twenty years there will definitely be an economic collapse in the U.S. similar to the economic setback that occurred in 2008. It is always good to have money handy. Make sure we have money handy because the banks will not readily provide loans. We should keep as much cash as possible on hand. We should not cash in our stocks. We will be able to ride out this economic collapse. It will last less than seven years, shorter than the last economic collapse.

If we wanted to invest our money in a safe and advantageous way, it would be to buy silver coins and not keep them in bank safe deposit boxes but instead kept safely in our homes. Buying silver coins is better than investing money in a bank. The value of silver will go up and make it profitable.

The Alliance is supporting the use of bitcoins. They are supporting bitcoms such as what is now being used in Africa. That is a positive thing. It can replace the use of world currencies.

## The USA in the near future

This country is going to have more than two political parties. A new party is at our threshold. The third party will emerge because one will break up and split into two.

There will be changes or modifications made to the second amendment of the U.S. Constitution regarding guns. New laws will be passed regarding the use of guns but the answer is not correct. They should not have done that. Too many people are here. There will be many guns that are not legal but there will be better control of guns.

The outcome of managing all the immigrants on our border will not be successful at first but it will be at the end. There will be many deaths and bloodsheds mainly because of the ignorance and stupidity of some of the people; some of the immigrants and some of the Americans.

Although the United States is now figuratively breaking up as a country, parts of this country will not become a totally different country in the far future.

There will not be a widespread electrical blackout in our country but blackouts will occur. Another country will get into our computer system that controls our electricity. That could be considered a form of warfare but it will not be dangerous and not controlling.

The Supreme Court will overturn Rowe versus Wade by modifying it. There will be a new abortion ruling. Nevertheless, illegal unrestricted abortions will continue. There will be different attitudes toward abortions in various states. The Court will not rule against homosexuality.

The debts that our government has incurred will not be lowered by reductions in Medicare and Social Security in the future. We will all be taken care of in that regard.

At this time the Republicans and the Democrats will not arrive at an agreement for a health insurance bill. What we call Obama Care will continue. Everybody will be taken care of and Americans will be able to get affordable health care for pre-existing conditions.

There will not be trials in our country in which thousands of government officials and workers and elected officials are sentenced to prison. There will not be many people sent to prison. It appears that there is a temptation to, but it is not going to happen.

There is as much racism in this country as the media portray and it will increase during the next ten tears.

Communism will never succeed.

## The political scene

President Biden will become mentally incompetent in the third year of his presidency and Kamala Harris will be the acting president until Biden's term ends. She will take the party further to the left. Biden will not seek the nomination again. Harris will be the Democrat Party nominee in the 2024 election.

The Republican candidate will win the election because many Democrat voters will vote Republican, not because they like what the Republican candidate stands for but because they are voting against what the Democrats have done during the preceding four years.

Donald Trump will not be nominated to run against Harris. The Republican candidate will be Mike Pence. He will make the correct decisions as president. He will serve two terms as president. There will not be more political harmony between the two parties during Pence's presidency but there will be during the term of his successor. The economy situation will worsen during Biden's presidency but it will be restored to what it is now during Pence's presidency.

His vice-president will not have been associated with Trump. His vice-president will be as good a president as he was. He will succeed Pence as president and will serve two terms. His presidency will end in 2040. There will be a third successive Republican president.

## Secret activities

There are secret societies composed of human beings that control much of the activities on the earth. There is much power with money, both benevolent and malevolent. Our country is run by mostly by certain behind the scene powers. It usually really does not matter who is elected president.

There is an organization in Bohemian Grove California that is composed of select individuals who decide who the next president will be but Donald Trump was not selected by them. He was selected by the people instead. The Bohemian Grove is an arm of the Cabal. They are very much opposed to Trump. This group is an extension of Skull and Bones of Yale University.

Planned Parenthood is a manipulation of society by the Cabal. The aborted fetuses are not always discarded. They are used by certain groups in their ceremonies, but they will be used for perfection, meaning they use them for experimentation and research.

Lady Gaga will change direction and seek to expose the Cabal and the harm they have done to her soul. It's like she sold her soul to the devil. She needed to be noticed. They promised her and they made her a star. She would not have gotten to the point where she is now if not for the Cabal. Selling your soul to the devil means allowing another entity or group to control you.

The universities in our country are being used to promote the One World Order. This is also true in the public school systems throughout the country.

The Cabal is in charge of our secret space program and is managed by the Rothschild family. The Rothschild family is one of thirteen families that are controlling the behind the scene powers.

Queen Elizabeth plays a significant role in what we call the Illuminati. The thirteen families that compose the Illuminati are really the behind the scene controllers of world events. For that reason, the royalties of the various families tend to intermarry to keep the blood lines pure. They are gradually losing control since they no longer always intermarry.

A man named G. E. Kincade found artifacts in the caves in the walls of the Grand Canyon and then the Smithsonian Museum removed them and denied their existence. They do not understand and they fearful that others will not understand. Those artifacts were of ancient human origin, not extraterrestrial. They left a record of their customs behind, a writing of their history for later humans to discover and learn.

The United States government regulates the price of gold, silver and diamonds.

We would be correct in fearing what the pharmaceutical companies are doing to mankind. They want money and they are making money. They want power and they have the power. The pharmaceutical companies exert tremendous influence on politics.

Project Mercury of the National Security Administration records telephone conversations of a large majority of Americans. We should be more careful of what we say in our telephone conversations. A wired phone in our homes is not safer than a cell phone.

Our government has the power to tamper with our memories. They have been able to erase certain memories from people, especially memories of secret government projects on which they have been working.

The government is experimenting with modifying the DNA of humans in a manner similar to what the Anunnaki have done. They are secretly experimenting with changing the DNA of humans.

In the project Stargate of the United States government, some people are successfully being trained to do remote viewing. The government is recruiting and training people for such. The Russians are well known for doing remote viewing but we are doing it also.

In 2001 Donald Rumsfeld said that more than two trillion dollars from the Department of Defense could not be accounted for. That money was secretly used for involvement in space.

The government uses mind control to cause people to do nefarious acts. Many people mindlessly do as the government bids. If the government wants a crime committed, they can put thoughts into a person's head to perpetrate that act. In reality, the mind cannot be controlled but can only be influenced. The exercise of a person's free will determines what the person will actually do.

The government intercepts applications for patents as soon as they are sent to the U.S. Patent Office to prevent certain inventions from becoming a reality such as those for free energy or for cures for diseases.

The government does not still store gold in the vaults at Fort Knox. Heroin or dangerous drugs, instead of gold is stored there. The gold that was stored in Fort Knox has been transferred to various underground places in Southeast Asia.

Recently it was announced that astronomers are getting a signal from a planet that is nine light years away from ours. Scientists are now backpedaling on that because there is a government conspiracy to keep quiet about it

In regard to our space program, the government has not gone back to the moon because something was discovered there that has caused fear to return.

In addition to providing health care, Obama care was designed by behind the scene powers as a means to control society. The Cabal is controlling the scene there. The belief is that if the government can control our health, they can eventually control many facets of our life, like even where we live or what kind of work we do. We are being manipulated. It is to our advantage to resist that manipulation.

Jesse Ventura is on the right path with his conspiracy theories. There is some basis or truth in most of the conspiracy theories that are circulating.

**Other countries now and in the near future**

The people in North Korea do not want to die. They are rooting for their mates in South Korea to be with them. The North Koreans will use an atom bomb, not on another country but rather in the ocean. The North Koreans are bluffing as much as our country is bluffing.

Relations between the United States and North Korea will eventually improve. They can open the door and communicate verbally. All the threats that were made will be dissolved. There will be no war.

North Korea will never detonate a nuclear bomb on another country. It will backfire on them. North Korea and South Korea will eventually be reunited. North Korea will become friends with our country. The leader in North Korea has a mishap in his brain. He is a young man who is really in love with himself. He will last as a leader but he will not be very successful. Nothing is going to happen to the leadership in North Korea.

Prince Charles will become the king of England for a very short time. He is a weakling but his son, Prince William, will absolutely be a good king and he will be king for a long period of time.

There is no concern about Saudi Arabia running out of oil. This is not going to occur. The Saudis do not tell and are not honest. We should not trust them. OPEC will continue to exist but there will be another name. Much more oil will be discovered in our country but it is not needed. The United States and Israel are energy independent now and will remain so.

The economic situation in Venezuela will get worse before it gets better. The Russians will try to get involved but will not succeed. Venezuela is not going to be invaded. There will be peace. The president will be in power as much as he can but he will not win in the end.

The Russians also are now planning an expedition to the moon and they will tell us that there are extraterrestrials on the moon waiting there. The Russians will expose them to the world. The extraterrestrials will have no need any more to disguise themselves. They will expose who they are and they won't frighten us.

Russian president Putin is not a secret ally of the United States. He has used chemical weapons on people of other countries at times.

Teresa May, the former British prime minister, was justified in expelling Russian diplomats recently for that reason. A lot of countries are justly retaliating against Russia.

There is a cold war now between the United States and Russia but we will not be enemies in the end. The two countries will be more closely aligned in the near future. They will exchange architecture. Mr. Putin is not completely aware of the Cabal.

Politically whichever way America goes, liberal or conservative, other countries in the world will follow.

Iran is experimenting with manipulating people's DNA so that those people will work against the enemies of Iran. They are so sneaky but that is their way of life. At the time that President Obama gave more than one billion dollars to Iran he was allied with them.

The islands that the Chinese are building in the sea do not have anything to do with stargates but there are UFO bases in the China Sea. The Chinese are doing much more than our government in regard to the exploration of space. They are far ahead of the United States. Their involvement with space exploration will help the Chinese inherit the earth. Extraterrestrials will help the Chinese. China is making a lot of inroads into Africa and they are taking over some of those countries.

China is building islands in the water to extinguish America. They are getting ready as Japan did on the American troops. We will increase our knowledge of water. In the sea and under the sea we will have many troops. It is not above the land. It is below the land that we must be mindful of. China secretly owns a lot of natural land resources in the United States such as New York and oil fields.

## Miscellaneous

In the year 1139 an Irish priest, Saint Malachy Morgain, had a vision about the Catholic popes. He said there would be 112 more popes and said things about those popes. Pope Francis is the 112th pope. The vision of Saint Malachy was correct in a way when he said that the 112th pope would signal the end of the power of the Vatican. The Catholic position is getting less in control but is very powerful. Pope Francis will be the last of the popes as such. The Catholic Church will continue for several thousand more years. Although the downfall of the Catholic Church is already in progress, it will continue in a different way. The Catholic Church will continue to do good and continue to have control.

By moving so far to the left and by exhibiting such hatred for President Trump and everything that he did, the Democrat party is dissolving itself. It will dissolve within a few of years. There will be another party coming through that will be much stronger. The Democrats are fearful. They know what is happening and they're trying to make the best of it. The new Democrat Party will not be a progressive party. It will be a more centrist party like the original Democrats, a much kinder; a much more stable party is coming through.

Our government and the governments of other countries are building huge or numerous underground cities.

The earth is likely to be struck by an asteroid in next twenty years but it won't have any serious effect.

# EVENTS OF THE FUTURE

## Planet changes

There will be an Earth shift in the next twelve thousand years such as when Atlantis virtually disappeared. The areas least affected will be all the places not near water. As Edgar Cayce said, the Virginia Beach area will be safe.

Global warming is a natural thing that is definitely going to occur. It includes weather changes of all kinds of different weather patterns, not just an increase of temperature. The answer to man's effect on global warming will be solved within the foreseeable future in a different direction from where we are going now.

Sea levels will rise to the point that many east coast cities of the United States will be inundated with water. One of the areas of the world that will be most seriously affected by the rising levels of the seas and oceans is Florida. Florida will be partly underwater but not before the turn of the century. Many other areas, especially Japan and Europe, will be affected. Significant effects of the rising sea levels in any other areas in the word will not be within the lifetimes of anyone alive today.

The most powerful volcanoes on Earth today are in the United States but they will never have a major effect on the development of humanity.

A huge emission of methane gas from thawing Arctic permafrost beneath the East Siberian Sea is a threat to mankind, but not in the near future.

The ice covering Antarctica will melt considerably in the next 1300 years.

We will see the rise of Atlantis within the next 6000 years.

In the year 3000 life on Earth in many ways will not be very different from what it is now.

## The Ascension

The Ascension has long been prophesized in many religions as an event of great magnitude that will change humanity forever. The Bible refers to the Ascension when it says that there will be a millennium of peace and "Two men shall be in the field; the one shall be taken, and the other left."

A thousand years, as in the Bible, is just a word that means an unending amount of time. At the time of the Ascension the planet will also undergo changes but will only affect the people in a positive way. Life will be much more peaceful on Earth after the Ascension. At the time of the Ascension approximately twenty-nine percent of the people will remain on Earth. Many will be what we would think of as just ordinary people.

A solar flash will not initiate the Ascension to push the earth from the third density to the fourth density. The Ascension was not the third secret that was given to the children at Fatima Portugal in 1917. It was pertaining to health. It is true as many ancient religions throughout the world have prophesized that there will be Ascension of humanity.

In the forthcoming Ascension when the earth and our entire solar system move from the third density to the fourth density, causing some humans to remain on Earth in the fourth density and others to be relocated on third density planets, the same will be true of those spirits now associated with the earth.

In the future when Earth experiences severe cataclysms and changes, a sizeable portion of the people will be rescued and placed aboard UFO's. It will be a little more than 10,000 years from now. We will go on to different planets but a few of us will remain. This is part of the Ascension.

At the time of the Ascension, people will the taken off Earth to two different planets in UFOs that use stargates. Conditions on those planets will be much the same as the now are on Earth. Before that time, humans will not have inhabited those planets.

People on those planets will evolve the same as they would have remained on Earth if the Ascension had not taken place. They will still have to deal with their karma.

There are now many people on Earth who are assisting in different ways in preparing for the Ascension. Psychics and mediums are assisting in the Ascension but hypnotists and medical doctors are not.

The people taken off planet will still experience the effects of their karma. The people who remain on Earth will be in lighter bodies of a higher vibrational level but they will still have a physical form. They will eat vegetables which will also be of a higher vibrational level. There will be no disease or crime but there will still be differences of opinions among people.

Only about thirty percent of the people will believe that the Ascension will occur.

After the Ascension socialism will be prevalent for those who remain on Earth but it will fail before that time.

No members of the Cabal will remain on Earth after the Ascension but 35 percent of the Alliance will.

President Trump will not be taken off planet. Presidents Obama Biden and Reagan are also highly advanced souls who will remain on Earth. All three had honest intentions. Neither of the two Bush presidents had honest intentions nor will they remain on Earth. Nancy Pelosi is a sincere person who will remain on Earth. Chuck Schumer is not sincere but will not remain on Earth after the Ascension. George Washington as well as the majority of the U.S. presidents were highly advanced souls. Twenty U.S. presidents will remain on Earth after the Ascension as well as future presidents.

## **Warfare and terrorism**

China will dominate the world economically within the next century because the people of China are very intelligent. They are currently working with extraterrestrials regarding their plan to overtake America. There will be a major economic struggle between China and the United States and the Chinese will win.

At this moment there are other countries with which we are in disagreement but there will not be any action such as war. Iran is insignificantly not knowledgeable regarding the detonation of an atomic bomb. They will attempt to use atomic warfare but they are very slow and lacking in knowledge. Iran will try to hit another country with a missile but it will not be successful.

Regarding atomic weapons, the country that we have most to fear from is ourselves.

North Korea is more limited than we think it is. North Korea will eventually become more cordial with our country and North Korea and South Korea will be united within twenty years from now (2021) and will become one country. North Korea will never bomb another country. It will backfire on them.

There will be no more wars in which uniforms are worn. We are at war at this moment but we won't have to worry about nuclear war.

There will be peace in Israel but there will also be a war of religions in which no atomic weapons will be used. As long as religions exist we will continue to have war.

We will have increasing racial battles in the streets of our country.

The radical Muslim movement is making a good point of its generation and the number of radicals will increase. It will still be here in 500 years and it will progress to be more of a threat.

Fifty years from now there will be more peace on Earth after more destruction. There will an alarming number of mass shootings, some of which will be by terrorists and some by domestics.

There is no country, not even America, which will be safe during the times that terrorism strikes.

Extraterrestrials will always protect us from having nuclear weapons for warfare. They will get directly involved to stop some countries from using nuclear weapons.

About thirty years ago China and Russia almost went to war with each other but they will not be adversaries again.

Israel will never use atomic weapons on another country.

An island which is part of Russia off the coast of Alaska will become part of the United States.

Guantanamo Bay prison in Cuba will not be used to house numerous people who will be charged with treason.

## America and international relations

Of all the countries, the most stable currency for the remainder of this century will be the U.S. dollar. Other forms of currency will also be accepted as currency in the United States. The paper dollar bill will disappear but paper bills of higher denominations will not disappear.

Speakers of Spanish will comprise more than one-third of the population of the United States. Our country will never have an official language.

The European Union will exist at least for 118 more years but will be broken up in different ways. The Euro will not decline in value but it will increase.

There will continue to be a cold war between the United States and Russia but it won't be any worse than it has been. Russia and the United States will eventually no longer be considered enemies.

America, but not the United States, will remain a dominant force in the world for at least eight centuries from now when China takes over. In regard to the international political situation, America will be very strong, very opinionated and will succeed.

The United States will not continue to exist as a country after five more centuries. It will evolve into another country with added territories. The United States is going to be the new Atlantis in many different ways and it will be more powerful and controlling. In a way, the people in America will take on the qualities of the ancient Atlanteans.

The physical features in Antarctica that remain from the time of Atlantis will emerge from the ice.

Some states in our country will make efforts to secede from the United States as several did states when Lincoln was president. Five states will be divided into several states: New Mexico, Texas, California, Florida and New York.

People mishandling guns will be an increasing problem.

The use of mind altering drugs will become a far more serious problem than it is now.

Wiki leaks will expose many Americans who are supporting the work of the Deep State.

## Society and religion

780 years from now, there will be much peace throughout the world and wars will be a thing of the past but there will always be confrontations among Earth people.

Women will become the dominant gender and will become leaders of the world.

Within the next century there will be large numbers of designer babies created; that is, selected DNA from more than two parents or even a community of parents.

Human society will never get past the point where the one with the most money rules and makes the rules and oppresses those that have less money.

Human nature is the reason that socialism as a form of government will never endure until after the Ascension.

In the next 400 years, Christians, Jews and Moslems will coexist peacefully without confrontations or warfare but in our lifetime we will still have wars. There will continue to be religious wars after many, many failures and many deaths.

Religion is slowly dissolving and it will no longer exist 6000 years from now. The big churches that now have very large congregations will become increasingly less significant. A major crisis or scandal in the Catholic Church will be exposed. In this century major changes will occur in many religions, not just Catholicism. The Cabal will exert increasing influence over our churches. The churches are being controlled by forces that are not necessarily beneficial to humans

Racial discrimination in our country will continue to exist for many centuries in the future. Racial integration will not occur in our country neither will peace. Racial discrimination is decreasing but will continue to exist.

There will be Marshall Law in our country to combat civil unrest in certain parts of the country but not in the entire country. We are going in the direction of the one world order that is propounded by the Cabal but it will not come into existence.

The third Jewish temple will be built 900 years from now in Jerusalem replacing the second temple that was destroyed in the year 70 A.D.

## Science and technology

The genetic manipulation of human DNA to create more advanced human beings by our scientists will become a reality in the next century. It is already in progress and they are experimenting with it. This will come to light in a very short time. Although it is being developed to be used in a harmless way it will turn out with some negativity.

Humans will be able to travel to the home planet of the extraterrestrials that helped build the pyramids.

The means of counteracting gravity obtained from crashed spaceships will be widely put to use in the next 3000 years.

The Doomsday Vault in Norway which stores the seeds of various varieties of vegetation will never be used in the event of an Earth catastrophe. It will be successful for humans to have this but it is not needed.

Humans will discover and take advantage of more abundant sources of energy than they now have.

Automobiles without wheels will run on our streets and highways by the end of this century.

It will be necessary for airplanes and helicopters to have another engine for safety reasons.

Within the lifetime of those alive today, the United States government will require microchips to be implanted in the skin of all newborn babies. Like animals, people will also be micro chipped for control and identification.

Written birth certificates will no longer be needed because they will be on microchips beneath the skin. This is an action influenced by the Cabal for control.

Within 3000 years, artificial humans will be virtually identical to biological humans. Women won't need men and likewise men won't need women. The time will never come when human-like robots will be self-reproducing.

The internet will continue to exist for many years to come but it will change radically from what it is now. The government will take increasing control over it and it will not be free. Within 60 years, humans will be implanted with devices under their skin that will directly connect them with the internet.

Telepathy is already occurring with the new generation and it will become a natural ability for a greater part of the population.

Within the next 50 years, mechanical robots will increasingly take over the functions of many activities that are now performed by humans to the point that human life will be very different from what it now is.

Free energy is slowly coming into existence but will not be accepted easily.

## Miscellaneous

There are major forces at work in many countries to create a one world government and it will occur on Earth after the Ascension.

Within the next 30 years we will have visual physical contact with extraterrestrials that are recognizably different from us.

As Edgar Cayce has stated, a chamber under one of the paws of the sphinx called the Hall of Records that contains a full account of the pre-history of humans will be discovered and exposed to mankind 107 years from now.

# EXTRATERRESTRIALS

NASA is withholding some very significant information from us regarding the universe and extraterrestrial life. They have a secret space program in addition to their publicized program. They have activities on Mars that they are not telling anyone about.

Our government has been spending much money each year for secret facilities and searching for extraterrestrial life. There is secret cooperation between our government and aliens.

The United States has military installations that house extraterrestrial beings who are in areas around us everywhere and the extraterrestrials change their location often.

There is an underground hidden city near Dulce, New Mexico in which thousands of extraterrestrials live under the cooperation and observation of the United States government. There has been a pact between the aliens and us there.

In addition to the installation in Dulce New Mexico, there are additional secret underground military installations in the United States. Extraterrestrials experiment on humans there and they share their technology with us and they keep up to their part of the agreement.

The reason for the security needed surrounding Area 51 in the air force base is because of the extreme secrecy. They are hiding information about aliens, UFOs, equipment, experiments and research.

There is a secret government installation beneath the Denver airport that does not involve extraterrestrials. That installation has been designed to be a place for our government to move to if Washington D.C. is no longer viable for such.

The HAARP facility in Alaska to control weather is a potentially dangerous experiment to the earth and mankind. No one can control anything that's going to happen regarding the weather. The danger will be when the people doing the experiment will drown. There is no extraterrestrial involvement there at this time but there will be a time that we will need help but not at the present.

Our government is using the HAARP facility in Alaska for experimental purposes, especially for mind control. There is much secrecy about the facility that the government is not publicizing.

Some of our technology has been achieved through analyzing equipment found on crashed UFO's that have been there for many years. The United States government is involved in programs of reverse engineering of alien spacecraft and other alien equipment. They examine what they have found and then cover it so it cannot be found.

There are people in our government, especially in Congress, but also in other parts of the government, who are extraterrestrials that look like Earth humans. All of them mean to help us and none mean to do us harm. Some of them do not know that they themselves are aliens.

Extraterrestrials are monitoring our nuclear facilities because they are concerned about the direction our civilization is taking. They are very curious and they wish to be in control because they are fearful of what we might do. There may be a potential for a nuclear war but they will not allow it to happen.

Israel has forces such as no man has created because they are being guided by a powerful extraterrestrial force.

The information in the U.S. government *Project Blue Book* about human encounters with extraterrestrials is completely accurate. It was declassified to make it seem as though it was not true, even though it was true. It is not the only true information that has been declassified. Sometimes the government declassifies information to make us believe it was false.

Extraterrestrials have considerable influence on American politics. Some groups influence one political party and other groups influence the other party. It is a proxy contest between different extraterrestrials groups.

All of the U.S. presidents, including Donald Trump, have knowingly had face-to-face contact with extraterrestrials, but they are fearful that they will be humiliated if they publicize that. It was because of his meetings with extraterrestrials that Trump created the Space Force. Extraterrestrials gave him information regarding the creation of the Space force. The relationship between the extraterrestrials and Trump was cordial, not at all adversarial. Most of those extraterrestrials looked just like humans but there were others who did not.

Extraterrestrials have already met President Biden. They are trying to convince him to come around to their way of thinking and are succeeding in doing so. He is a sincere president and his thinking is changing and he will be a better president because of this.

Adam and Eve were extraterrestrials who could be described as super humans who came to Earth to infuse their DNA with that of the humans on Earth at that time.

Some of the royal lines of kings and queens originated with extraterrestrial involvement. Some are descended from alien beings and some are part alien and part human.

Epidemics or plagues that have affected humans have been caused by microbes on meteorites and asteroids that have hit the earth deliberately sent by extraterrestrials. Some diseases in humans today, mostly those of a neurological nature, were caused by extraterrestrials.

The Atlanteans were hybrids of humans and extraterrestrials as we are.

The origin of the system of priests in various religions was humans who were able to communicate with extraterrestrials and act as intermediaries between them and Earth people. Aaron, the brother of Moses, was one such person. He was not well liked by the people.

Babies with reptilian features are sometimes born of human mothers who have had sexual contact with extraterrestrials.

Since the appearance of humans on Earth, including the present time, there have been both good and evil extraterrestrials attempting to direct the evolution of mankind on Earth. Currently there are many more with good intentions than with evil intentions.

Extraterrestrials imbue some of their own attitudes and desires into the DNA of humans to make humans more like them. Opposing groups of extraterrestrials have spliced some of their own DNA into different groups of humans in the past and are still doing so.

The imbued DNA is passed on from generation to generation. That is a major cause of the wide political division in our politics today.

The division between the Democrats and the Republicans was in our ancient past and it started with opposing extraterrestrial groups about 500,000 years ago.

The Gulf Stream was engineered by extraterrestrials to bring warm waters to what is now northern Europe.

Up to 60,000 years ago, some extraterrestrials who visited the earth encouraged animal sacrifices. Those traditions were continued in some religions, including the religion of Abraham.

The manipulation of the weather by extraterrestrials was used as a weapon in warfare in the past.

In 1990 and 1991 extraterrestrials caused worldwide nuclear weapon programs to cease to function for a period of time because they were trying to stop our work with atomic energy. We will never have a nuclear war because extraterrestrials that watch over the earth will not permit it. Atomic warfare on Earth could damage our entire solar system.

Our planet has a defense grid around it that was erected by extraterrestrials to protect us and not allow entry of negative extraterrestrials into our atmosphere.

Most of the mysterious ancient structures found on Earth today were built by extraterrestrials for their own activities rather than for the use by or the good of humans.

Thirteen ancient elongated crystal skulls found in Egypt and in the Americas were of alien origin and have very powerful energy. When those skulls are brought together, great power will be given to the extraterrestrials that made them. There are also other objects located on Earth that are endowed with powers.

Aliens were involved in the construction of the Coral Castle in Homestead, Florida to help Edward Leedskalnin.

The architects and builders of the pyramids in the Yucatan and Guatemala were built more than 10,000 years ago by those of another star system, the Pleiadians, the most advanced extraterrestrials involved in Earth activities. They built pyramids in Egypt that they could reach from the top down. Humans provided the labor in the construction but extraterrestrials provided the technology.

There are numerous very long lines, drawings of animals, geometrical shapes and mathematical diagrams that can only be seen from the air in South America. Their purpose was that those up high in the sky could read them easier. They were constructed by extraterrestrials 9800 years ago for the purpose of providing instructions or information to the people of Earth.

The same could be said about the various crop circles that have been appearing throughout the world. They are messages from extraterrestrials. We should investigate the crop circles and seek to interpret them.

Extraterrestrials were involved in the formation of the Devil's Tower in Wyoming 8100 years ago.

The dress of Betty Hill, who claims she and her husband were abducted by aliens in 1961 contains DNA evidence from an extraterrestrial.

The ancient astronauts that are depicted in stone carvings throughout the world are both extraterrestrials and human time travelers from our future. More than 100,000,000 time travelers from our future are on Earth today, as well as 7000 time travelers from our past.

There are ruins of whole cities on Earth both on the land and in the waters that were built by extraterrestrials; some more than 200,000 years ago.

The Dogu (Dogoo) statues found in Japan represent aliens in space suits.

There are extraterrestrials on Earth not only from star systems in our galaxy but from other star systems in other galaxies as well.

Extraterrestrials are now as active on our planet as they were a thousand or so years ago and the time is coming that they will show themselves. Extraterrestrials that looked different from humans openly lived with humans on Earth 70,000 years ago.

Nowadays there are some extraterrestrials living on Earth who look different from humans but most extraterrestrials look exactly like Earth people. Those that don't look like humans are underground and in the ocean or in caves but not openly on the surface of the earth. There are extraterrestrials that we call ant people who look like us but have heads that look like the heads of ants.

There are extraterrestrials that can show themselves in the physical to people on Earth as something different from what they actually are, much the same as angels do.

Shape shifters are aliens disguised as humans. There are no specific features that we can look for to identify them. They are not dangerous to humanity.

There is what is often referred to as "little people" from other systems living in isolated places on Earth and there are also tall giant people.

What we call "Black Eyed Children" are extraterrestrials who cause damage and distress.

There is a connection between the Grand Canyon and star beings as thought by Native American Indians in that area.

There are 291 undersea UFO bases on the earth.

Hitler played a predestined role in our history and was guided by extraterrestrials, the same group of extraterrestrials that assists the Taliban and the ISIS today.

Long ago some ancient extraterrestrials sought to have humans worship them as gods.

Extraterrestrials on Earth today are nearly all of a positive nature but a few are of a negative nature.

There is a large system of caves in the state of Washington in which more than 16,000 people from other planets live.

At the present time, there is no one star system that has more influence on the activities on Earth than other star systems. They are working as a unified group and are not in conflict with each other.

Mathematics is used as the basic form of communication because sometimes it is easier using mathematics. It provides a universal means of communication between those on Earth and physical entities in every civilization in other worlds.

Extraterrestrials were the cause of the numerous mutilizations of animals across America in recent years in which certain organs had been surgically removed for research.

People have been abducted by extraterrestrials for sexual experimentation and breeding; some do not remember what occurred.

Extraterrestrials sometimes abduct the consciousness or minds of people without abducting their bodies. Extraterrestrials are no longer experimenting with Earth people but they are still abducting them for positive reasons. They are interested in upgrading their DNA as they have been doing for hundreds of thousands of years.

Extraterrestrials have abducted humans and implanted devises beneath their skin for sending information back to them, and also for manipulating and controlling those who have been abducted.

There are extraterrestrials who are interested in getting gold from our planet. It is easier to find gold on our planet than it is on other planets.

Extraterrestrials were instrumental in providing information for the design of the St. Louis Arch to have an effect on the weather in that region.

The research and information presented on You Tube by Barbara Lamb regarding extraterrestrials and their interaction with humans is very credible. The same is true of David Wilcock.

There is an intergalactic federation composed of various extraterrestrial groups with an intergalactic council of nine that oversees or dictates the course of humanity on Earth.

Extraterrestrials have placed artificial satellites that orbit around the earth for our protection and for providing information about what is happening on Earth.

The Van Allen radiation belt that surrounds the earth was placed there by extraterrestrials.

The Chinese are doing much more than our government in regard to the exploration of space. Their involvement with space exploration will help the Chinese inherit the earth. Extraterrestrials are helping the Chinese at this moment.

Alien marine life forms exist in the deepest part of the oceans under hundreds of pounds of pressure.

There is much hidden information about the town Paradise, California which was destroyed by fire. 800 extraterrestrials from Alpha Centauri had a treaty with the humans there that permitted them to have a safe haven and live there peacefully because they were kind people and were nearly identical to humans. The fire was created and enhanced by laser beams by the Cabal to destroy the Centaurians because they were on the verge of disclosing their existence to the public.

The intent of the alien beings that we call the Grays is to exert great influence on human life on Earth.

The Aztec Indians worshipped the extraterrestrial Quetzalcoatl whom they believe to be a god.

Many of the ancient Sumerian gods were actually extraterrestrial beings. Nearly all of the world's great religions today came about as the result of encounters with extraterrestrials. Jehovah was an extraterrestrial who gave the Ten Commandments directly to Moses and still guides and protects the Jews in modern times.

Although the great percentage of extraterrestrials is benevolent, the lizard-like extraterrestrials are usually not.

Many of the gods portrayed in the various mythologies throughout the world were actually extraterrestrial entities. There is some truth in the foundation of mythology even though it is distorted. Much of the ancient mythologies regarding the various gods and goddesses are actually references to aliens who visited the earth.

Gods like Zeus or Jupiter were extraterrestrials. Long ago people believed that gods lived on the top of Mount Olympus but they were actually extraterrestrials that made their home there. In ancient times there were wars on the earth or in the skies above the earth between opposing groups of extraterrestrials which were often portrayed in various mythologies. There was not a physical war that we call the Clash of the Titans between Zeus and his siblings.

There is factual historical significance in the American Indian mythologies which often portray beings that are part ants and part humans.

The early Egyptian pharaohs were extraterrestrials or their descendants who were the offspring of extraterrestrials and humans. Queen Nefertiti in ancient Egypt was an extraterrestrial who showed herself as an Earth human with an elongated skull. The same is true of the Egyptian King Akhenaton. The ancient Egyptians tried to erase all evidence of the existence of Queen Nefertiti and King Akhenaton because they changed their religion from being polytheistic to monotheistic. King Akhenaton and Queen Nefertiti were the parents of Moses. He took that information back to the Jews and it became the foundation of the Jewish religion.

George Washington received alien intelligence during the Revolutionary War that helped him win the war.

There is truth in what Erich Von Daniken has written in his book *Chariots of the Gods.* It was information that was channeled to him by spirits.

Extraterrestrials do not have disease because they are in a higher dimension and we have disease because we are in a lower dimension.

Highly advanced extraterrestrial civilizations have imbued robots with some level of consciousness.

There are underground facilities at Rudloe Manor in England that are used for extraterrestrial research.

All extraterrestrials are capable of creating physical objects by simply using their minds, the same as spirits can do.

The information that Corey Goode presents on You Tube is worth our interest.

Extraterrestrials can erase specific memories from our minds.

Artificial spheres, some as large as our moon, come into our solar system to investigate.

The United States has recovered two UFO's in addition to the one discovered in area 51 in 1947. There was one crash before and one crash after the crash in 1947. We have gotten technology from the last two crashes. The government is not aware of the first crash. The third crash occurred in 1994 about 24 miles from San Francisco, California and was not publicized. Scientists know about it but not government officials.

UFO's will play a significant role in our country in the next 100 years. Thirteen people from the United States will enter UFO's of their own accord in the next 100 years. These incidents will not be reported to the public. 96 people will be taken forcibly into UFO's in the next 100 years. 18 of these incidents will be publicized and the majority of people will believe that is true. The reporting of those incidents will create worry by the population.

The purpose of the abductions will not be for manipulating DNA or for mind control but rather to learn about human anatomy in order to help humans with health problems. 59 percent of the abductions will be made by extraterrestrials that look just like humans. All of those abducted will be in great fear but they will all be returned unharmed and not have psychological problems afterward. They will consider it a negative experience.

There are about 9,000,000 extraterrestrials in our country that look just like humans. There are millions of extraterrestrials in the earth's spirit world.

Extraterrestrials compose one half of one percent of those in the earth's spirit world. Less than one percent of extraterrestrial are not benevolent in regard to Earth people.

Benevolent extraterrestrials do not always overpower those that aren't. Some malevolent extraterrestrials are extremely powerful and will overcome those who work for good purposes.

There are varying levels of intelligence among the different groups of extraterrestrials. Earth humans are the least intelligent. The overall level of the inhabitants of a planet is related to the extent of time that they have been there. The inhabitants of Earth are less intelligent that those on other planets because they have been on the planet for a shorter amount of time than those on other planets.

All extraterrestrials have the same five senses and what we call the sixth sense as Earth people have. Some have more than just six senses. The sense of taste is stronger in Earth people than it is in most extraterrestrials because it was given to them to help make them better slaves.

Like Earth humans, all extraterrestrials go through the reincarnation process for the same reasons that Earth people reincarnate. Like Earth humans, they reach a point where they no longer need to reincarnate. At that point, they are what we consider to be Christ spirits; that is spirits who have reached a level that reincarnation is no longer necessary.

When there is no longer a need to reincarnate, all entities reside in the spirit world of their particular moon or planet until they move on to a higher realm than the spirit world.

Extraterrestrials often come to Earth in UFO's and then reside among us without being recognized as extraterrestrials. A few living on Earth are malevolent. The percentage of extraterrestrials living among us will decrease in the future because the level of humanity will have been raised.

The simian family and humans are genetically related because those of the simian family were offshoots of humans created by the Anunnaki. Like other animals, they can reincarnate as humans or as animals.

## The Anunnaki

The Anunnaki are people on a different planet, what some call the tenth planet in our solar system. It is part of our solar system.

There were bi-peds that were indigenous to our planet before the intervention of the Anunnaki who came and changed them. They designed the human body to look like them by infusing their DNA into them. When the Bible said "Then God said, Let us make mankind in our image, in our likeness." that was actually in reference to the Anunnaki creating humans in their image. Both the human mind and the human body have been expanded with the infusion of DNA of the Anunnaki; more the body than the mind.

The Anunnaki began their work to create beings on Earth just like themselves about 5,000,000 years ago. They modified the bi-peds on Earth in order to have them serve as their slaves for the purpose mining gold which they needed restore their atmosphere.

The various types of humans such as the Neanderthal man, the Cro-Magnons etc. were created by the Anunnaki as prototypes that led to the development of the modern Homosapiens. They were models of humans created as an aid to them.

The cause of the apparent leap in human consciousness from the Neanderthal man to the Homosapiens was an infusion of the Anunnaki DNA into the Neanderthal man. It was because of the Anunnaki that the Neanderthals died out and the Homosapiens survived. The Neanderthals weren't able to evolve to the level that Homosapiens are able to evolve. However, there are still full-bred Neanderthals on the earth today in hidden enclaves in the caves in southern Spain.

The Anunnaki are very much involved in the creation of the next human species after the Homosapiens that some people refer to as the Homonoeticus which will fully appear in about 100,000 years. They will continue to improve human races after the Homonoeticus. Many million years from now they will get to the point where improvement is no longer needed when Earth beings not only look like them but will also be exactly like them.

The Anunnaki used a spaceship to travel from their home planet to Earth. They did not use any type of vortex or wormhole to travel here. They are on Earth now.

Although the Anunnaki had a great influence on the development of Earth humans, they are not our friends even though they continue to play a role protective of mankind on Earth.

The Draco extraterrestrials are the same as what Zechariah Sitchin called the Anunnaki. They are the force behind the Illuminati and are associated with the Cabal.

If the Anunnaki had not come to Earth, there would be no human life on Earth today and the animals would eventually reincarnate as humans elsewhere.

The Anunnaki manipulated the DNA of Earth humans to deactivate the function of the appendix to greatly shorten the lifetime limit. That required the humans to have more incarnations than if they had lived longer.

The function of the appendix will be restored by the manipulation of DNA by extraterrestrials; not by the Anunnaki but by another group.

There is just one race that is opposed to what the Anunnaki are doing in this regard. The two races have been struggling with each other for millions of years but one cannot be considered good and the other considered evil.

Zachariah Sitchin was correct when he said that Anunnaki rulers lived more than 20,000 years as well as some who weren't rulers.

The Anunnaki have not created humans on other planets as they did on Earth but other extraterrestrial groups have done things on other planets similar to what the Anunnaki did on Earth.

# HUMANS

## Consciousness

The most basic level is the everyday waking consciousness. There are several additional levels of consciousness. The deepest is the soul. The levels of consciousness from the deepest to the awake or surface level awaking consciousness are as follows: the soul, the higher self, the superconscious, the subconscious, the preconscious and surface level conscious.

The following information is not necessarily in keeping in keeping with that of the experts. The major levels of consciousness include the following:

1. The surface level consciousness is our everyday waking consciousness. It includes our thoughts and what we perceive about the world around us through our senses.

2. The pre-conscious level includes everything we ever knew in this lifetime. All the information that was once known but is now forgotten is stored in the preconscious. Anything that a person experiences or senses is stored in the preconscious as well as in the deeper levels of consciousness. Desires reach this level although the capacity to have desires (i.e. free will) is at the soul level.

3. The subconscious level is the point from which our thoughts, emotions and senses are generated. It is the source of our surface level consciousness. Our thoughts come from our subconscious before they come to our conscious mind.

Therefore the wording of the questions asked of a pendulum does not have to be correct because the pendulum picks up the intent of our thoughts from the subconscious.

4. The super conscious is a much deeper level than the subconscious. It is the source of our subconscious. It is the bridge between the higher self and the sub-conscious.

5. The deepest level that can be accessed is the higher self. Both humans and spirits have access to their higher self and the higher selves of others because the higher selves of all people are all connected. It includes information about some, but not all, of our previous incarnations. It is the source of our super-conscious. The pendulum can be a tool to access information from the higher self and the higher selves of others. Psychics are able to access higher selves without the use of a pendulum and can obtain more extensive information than can be attained by a pendulum. Anything in the higher self has the potential to be accessed through hypnotism.

6. No entity, even a person's higher self, can consciously receive information from the soul level. Our soul includes our intuition and everything that exists or ever existed or potentially ever will exist. It includes everything that ever occurs, occurred, or will occur. It includes all the information about ourselves including all our incarnations; past, present and future. It is the source of our higher self. It also includes the God element and is animated by the God force. It is eternal and cannot be destroyed.

Emotions are part of all levels of consciousness. Thoughts emanate at the soul level and can be located at any level of consciousness. A person's thoughts can be received through telepathy. Very often when you think of someone, there is telepathic communication between the two of you and there will very likely be an event involving the two of you in the near future.

Humans connect with all other humans as well as with extraterrestrials at all levels of consciousness except at the most basic level of the soul.

Carl Jung was not completely correct when he defined the universal consciousness because he included some of the attributes of what we call the higher self in his definition.

**Free will**

Free will is unrestricted desires without limits. Anything can be desired, but external conditions may be such that desires may not be able to be achieved because of restrictions placed upon the individual by an outside source. However circumstances can change a person's desires and subsequent actions based on those desires.

When a question is asked involving the exercise of a person's free will of a past action, the answer given by a pendulum will always be correct; but when the question is about a future action the answer will usually, but not always, be correct. Free will is a permanent part the soul, one of the elements of the higher self.

There are destinies in our lives that are determined before we reincarnate but those destinies do not necessarily have to come true. They are opportunities that are presented to us; the outcomes of which depend on the exercise of our free will.

## Spells and attachments

A person can cast a spell on another person. When the person who has cast the spell dies and goes into the spirit world, the spell is removed. Spells can be either negative or positive. Spirits can also cast spells on humans.

An entity can cast a spell on a person even if a person does not want a spell cast at the conscious level. The person on whom the spell has been cast cannot remove the spell but the person or spirit who cast the spell can remove it. No other humans or spirits can remove the spell but they can assist in removing it by projecting thoughts into the mind of the person who cast the spell.

A person can cast a spell on another person by using an object such as a doll and sticking pins into it. Spirits can cast spells on a person at the subconscious level.

Karma is created for the person or spirit who casts a spell.

No one can remove a spell for someone else but Jesus cast spells from many people but it was the Christ spirit that dwelt in him that did so.

Spells cannot be cast on spirits but they can be cast on animals. Animals cast spells on people as well as on other animals.

Spells cast on a person are not the same as attachments. Attachments are always negative. They are entities unto themselves that are not created by spirits but rather by the person himself because at the subconscious level he wanted it. Attachments are caused because of anger or vengeance. They cannot drive a person insane.

Attachments can be placed anywhere on the body and, for example; an attachment placed on the heart could cause heart problems. An attachment on the brain could affect a person's thinking.

A person's mind cannot be affected by other entities or make the person insane unless the person wants that at the subconscious level.

56 percent of humans have attachments that they have placed on themselves.

## Sexual activity

Sexual activity is a spiritual activity as well as a physical activity for both people and animals. It can take people to a higher level of spirituality but only for the moment.

It makes no difference if the activity is between two people of the same sex or two people of the opposite sex. It is designed to be pleasurable for both humans and extraterrestrials so that they would engage in such activities for procreation and spiritual enlightenment as well as simply for pleasure.

It would not be healthy for a person to intentionally abstain from sex for a period of time unless there was a health issue. Religion should promote sexual activity rather than promoting abstinence. Many priests would be better priests if they were married. The percentage of homosexual priests is higher than the percentage of men in the general population. There are many homosexual priests who are priests because they want to abstain from sexual activities.

Spirits have nothing that resembles the sexual activities similar to those of humans.

All extraterrestrial groups include sexual activities in which the norm involves just two people. No extraterrestrial group reproduces by means other than sex between two people unless cloning is considered otherwise. Normal activities do not include more than two individuals.

Cloning was a prevalent method in previous civilizations and will also be so in future civilizations. The soul enters a cloned body the in the same manner it does in a naturally conceived body.

Whether or not they appear as humans or differently, the bodies of all extraterrestrials are either male or female similar to the concept of those of Earth humans. There is no other kind of body design other than male or female in any other extraterrestrial group.

An excessive libido is not spiritually detrimental. Excessive sexual activities can be detrimental only to the body but not the spirit.

It is a negative effect of natural laws when humans engage in sexual activities with animals. The same is usually true when one species of animal engages in such activities with another species.

Extraterrestrial humans that look like Earth humans frequently mate with Earth humans and produce offspring. There are no problems involved in such mating. Sexual activity between humans and extraterrestrials is more common that realized. There are about 2,000,000 offspring of such mating living on Earth today. Those offspring usually mature in various ways differently from the mating of two Earth humans. Although they do not usually have difficulty in adjusting to life on Earth, they think differently.

After the Ascension when people are in lighter bodies, people will continue to reproduce in the same manner as they now do.

In the civilizations before Atlantis, reproduction was by the same means as it now does. Both people and animals in the very earliest of Earth civilizations reproduced in the same manner as in the present.

The Bible condemns male homosexuality because religion dictates that sperm should not be wasted. Nothing in the Bible is said about female masturbation. Masturbation by males and females is permissible within the laws of nature by both humans and animals. Masturbation does not harm the soul. Masturbation can be harmful to humans if mind altering drugs are used. If not using drugs, a person cannot excessively masturbate unless there is a health issue.

Three percent of people more than 100 years old engage in sexual activities. Fifteen percent of people over the age of 100 years old are capable of sexual activity but do not engage in such but wish they would.

## Humans before Homosapiens

In the ancient past there were several types of humans on Earth at the same time, including Neanderthals and Homosapiens etc. The human race, both the Neanderthals and the Homosapiens, first appeared on Earth in Africa. The Neanderthal humans and Homosapiens did not coexist peacefully but there was no warfare between them. They had different opinions and were of equal, but different, intelligence. The Homosapiens outlasted the Neanderthals because it was time for the Neanderthals to no longer exist. The Ice Age affected the development and physical appearance of the Neanderthals. The skin color changed. The volcanic ash of approximately 39,000 years ago had an effect on the demise of the Neanderthals.

The origin of the different human races based on skin color on Earth was not related to the activities of various extraterrestrial groups. They absolutely had no influence on the development of the human races based on skin color although the Anunnaki influenced the existence of all races such as the Neanderthals and the Homosapiens. There was only one human race before the Great Flood.

The different races based on color developed from the influence of climate and weather rather than anything else. The current human races began in Africa and were all originally black and then the skin color and other physical differences changed as a result of their migration destinations. We were all here together and then went in different directions and became different races. Now the different races are blending and are becoming more similar.

There was a time when reptilian physical characteristics were prevalent in a large portion of Earth people. There are still such people on Earth living underground.

The early humans communicated by a very elementary form of telepathy. Language was first given to those that were able to communicate by sounds and grunts and sounds of pleasure. Spoken language gradually evolved and became a more efficient means of communication. There was originally just one spoken language rather than the proliferation of languages that exist in the world today. When we separated and went different ways, many different languages began to emerge.

There is a significant degree of accuracy in the writings of Damon T. Berry in his work called *The Knowledge of the Forever Time*.

The many prehistoric drawings of humans with birdlike heads throughout the world show that such beings did exist on Earth at one time. They were drawings of Earth inhabitants.

It was solely for extraterrestrial observation and their travel that the ancient humans placed so much focus on astronomy by building a great number of observatories throughout the world.

There was atomic warfare on Earth in ancient times before the Great Flood.

The American Indians were originally just one race of people that went in different directions and then separated into various tribes. They originated in Asia and then migrated to Alaska and then to South America. The American Indians are the physical descendants of the Atlanteans. They look more like the Atlanteans than do the other races.

Some early Earth humans were only three feet tall. They still exist on Earth today and live together in enclaves mostly underground.

**Humans in the future**

New humans are coming into existence and will be doing so for eternity. The information in this section refers specifically to those who currently exist. Some of the information also applies to those who come into existence throughout eternity.

Star children are the forerunners of a new race of humans, the Homonoeticus, which will eventually replace Homosapiens who will be more evolved. Humanity is evolving to a higher level through the entry of star children currently being born on Earth. They will be able to see the future, communicate without talking and will be very psychic.

When the Chinese government recently made a study of more than 100,000 children with unusual abilities, they were star children. Star children are very bright, intelligent and wise. They are more highly evolved souls than most souls and they have much confusion within. Jesus was a star child. So was Mohammad. So was Confucius. So was Sondra Zecher.

The Millennials and those born after the year 2000 are more advanced than the baby boomers. They are also very intuitive. As time proceeds a greater percentage of the population will be more psychic than at present.

Indigo children are brilliant, intelligent and very superior star children who are quite mystical. They are aware of the past and they are aware of the future. Indigo children are neither an increasing percentage nor a decreasing percentage of all the babies being born today.

Most of us use less than fifteen percent of our brain but as humans evolve, we will be using a greater part of our brain.

Humans are getting more in touch with psychic capabilities. We are going to get to the stage where people cannot lie to each other or when we can tell when we are being lied to. Most of us are liars. We even lie to ourselves or "fib" as we often say in order to lessen the intensity of the lie.

The genetic manipulation of human DNA to create a more advanced human being by scientists will become a reality in the near future.

Humans are gradually evolving into Grays in a different way. We will look somewhat more like the Grays and will be more like them thousands of years from now.

Humans will eventually communicate through telepathy rather than by spoken language as some already do. In the future only telepathy will be used. Telepathy is more efficient than spoken language.

Women will become the dominant gender taking more leadership roles in different areas of the world.

Marriage will become less significant or popular within the next hundred years. A smaller percentage of the population will be married. Only those who bear children will be married.

The average life span of a human being will increase by more than twenty years within the next few centuries. Humans will be living more than one hundred twenty years.

The use of our minds will slowly replace the use of much of our technology.

Those of us on Earth now will evolve into a spirit state and we will no longer be separated in matter. Incarnation will not be necessary but rather a matter of choice.

As humans evolve to a lighter density, we will be able to see things such as ghosts or cloaked UFO's that are currently beyond the range of perception of most people.

We are absolutely in the process of the acceleration of the Ascension right now, going from the third density to the fourth density. Those who evolve to the fourth density will have far greater abilities.

Those who remain on Earth after the Ascension will not have to speak different languages because we will read each other's minds just as even now we often communicate with people just by thinking about them.

## After the human state

When we are no longer required to reincarnate, we will remain on the astral plane indefinitely or eventually move to a higher realm or to a lower realm, wherever we wish. After we have reached the level of evolution where we are no longer required to remain in the spirit realm, we cast off our spirit bodies much the same as we cast off our physical bodies when we enter the spirit world. After spirits cast off their spirit form, some go to a higher realm and others are left back and have to come back into the physical for further learning.

No one from the human kingdom or from the spirit kingdom will ever become an angel but we can evolve to a state that we are like angels, as what is commonly called the "masters". There are 73 masters. Very few of us will reach the "angel state".

The goal of all humans and spirits is to go up to higher and higher realms of existence above that of spirits. There is potential for humans to eventually evolve to a level above that of the angels, evolving to a higher plane of existence.

All souls manifest themselves in various stages in their upward evolution such as the physical human body, the spirit form as well as various cosmic entities such as planets, moons, stars etc. It is a natural course of events that we can eventually evolve to the point that we become stars. All the billions of stars out there are souls that have gone through the process of being a human first.

Humans have the potential of eventually evolving to a level much further than we can now conceive, further than even cosmic entities.

## Worlds above the astral realm

After an entity no longer has a need to reincarnate and resides in the spirit world, they eventually move on to a higher level than the spirit world; what Theosophists call the mental world. This is a very personal world in which there are no interpersonal relationships. The entity is complete in itself but can have involvement of others.

The entity does not have emotions but it does have free will. There are worlds above the mental world. It can take millions of years from the time a person leaves the physical world to the time he enters the mental world. An entity can live in the mental world for millions of years before moving on. There exists what we call seven heavens; the levels of human evolution. The physical world is what is considered one of the seven heavens. This information is considered consistent with the material presented by Helena Blavatsky, the founder of the Theosophical movement.

## Miscellaneous

Natural, cataclysmic events such as comets or meteors played a major role in forming human civilization.

The Aryan race began in Siberia and migrated westward to Europe.

There aren't any planets or moons in our solar system in which there are inhabitants who are less evolved than Earth humans. Earth humans are the least evolved of any humans in our galaxy because they are the least informed. They are not able to comprehend what is given to them because they are limited. There are entities on other planets that are observing Earth humans and they like to give advice to them.

At the present time most extraterrestrials are desirous of helping Earth humans to evolve to a higher level.

# THE HUMAN BODY

## Nutrition

At times genetically engineered vegetables such as corn are harmful to your health. It will improve in the future because they will use less germicide.

Eating organically grown fruits and vegetables is significantly better for your health than eating most of the fruits and vegetables that are sold in supermarkets. For years and centuries before, people were eating fruits and vegetables and they survived well. Now we give it a new name, organically grown. We use a lot of chemicals and fertilizers to make them grow better. We would do better to eat fruits and vegetables that haven't been treated by chemicals.

It is better to eat food that has been grown near where we live rather than to eat food that comes from far away if we are eating fresh food.

Eating meat is a reflection of lower level consciousness. You can definitely raise your level of consciousness by avoiding red meat. Some meats are more harmful to the body than are other meats. Eating red meat is not beneficial to your health. Before the end of 2200 years from now, humans will no longer eat the flesh of animals.

For those of you who now continue to eat meat, it is better for your health to eat the meat of animals that have been fed organically grown food. The meat from buffalo is less harmful to your bodies than the meat from cattle. Beef is harmful but all kinds of liver are the most harmful. Chicken and turkey are among the least harmful meats.

Fish and fowl are more preferable to eat than the meat of four-legged animals. Fish are the least harmful. Shellfish can be harmful but not if eaten in moderation. Alaskan Pollack that is used to make imitation crab meat is not harmful. Seaweed is a food that would be beneficial to add to your daily diet.

There is a danger in drinking filtered water because doing so will leach out essential minerals and trace elements from your body. Drinking filtered water is not really a good thing. Although many people believe that drinking bottled spring water is better for your health than drinking the water that is piped into your homes, that is usually not correct. Regarding whether drinking alkaline water is good for your health, it depends upon who is drinking it. It will help some bodies to be less acidic.

It is possible for humans to exist on a type of green algae for nutrition, but not solely. There are natural grasses that will help us.

For many people, drinking a glass of wine each day would be beneficial to their health. A glass of wine and also a glass of water would be of benefit.

In regard to whether raw plant based foods can help cure cancer and other diseases more effectively than cooked plant based foods, it depends on the individual.

Wheat has been used as a weapon by the Cabal. It has been genetically modified to affect the thyroid gland so that people become less productive and more easily controlled. That is why people often become very sleepy after eating wheat. Other foods have also been modified for similar purposes. It would benefit you if you ate only organically grown foods.

## Herbs, drugs and supplements

For everyone the daily intake of 25 grams of Vitamin C would be beneficial for improving the immune system. There is no danger of taking too much vitamin C.

Vitamin B12 helps improve memory. Simply inhaling the fumes from vitamin B12 is less effective that vitamin B-12 pills. B-12 has a much better effect when it is injected.

To improve their memory, anyone with memory problems should drink tea made from the leaves of the marjoram herb. It would be a cure for many of those with dementia but not with Alzheimer's disease. It would help people with other problems as well but not with psychological problems. It is not recommended that everyone drink marjoram tea simply because some people do not need it.

Homemade humus with no additives can help cure or lessen the effects of Alzheimer's disease.

There are other teas that you are not aware of that can help people with health problems. Cinnamon tea could be helpful. Teas made from other spices and herbs would be helpful. No teas could be made that would be particularly good for the liver or kidneys. You are aware of the majority of the helpful teas.

Lavender is a tea good for headaches. Health supplements such as turmeric, green tea and aloe are healthful to the body. Herbs found on Earth and other natural remedies absolutely exist for curing all human diseases. Attempt to include a variety of herbs and spices in your diet.

It is not good to stand in front of a microwave oven while in use. Eating food or drinking a liquid that has been heated in a microwave oven can be detrimental to your health. You should avoid heating foods or liquids in a microwave oven if possible. When the microwave oven is in operation, stand further than three feet away from it.

Hemp oil or marijuana helps with pain caused by cancer. There can be very limited use of marijuana for people who have illnesses where you wouldn't be smoking enough to do any damage to your lungs. One doesn't have to smoke. It is only a plant and all medications come from plants. There are different parts of marijuana that are good for some illnesses.

The use of marijuana can take a person to a higher level of thinking or to a lower level. Even a controlled or limited use of marijuana can be as detrimental to a person's health as smoking cigarettes is. If you smoke marijuana it will have the same effect on your lungs and arteries as cigarettes but then there are situations that marijuana is helpful while cigarettes are never.

Mind expanding plants like magic mushrooms, peyote, San Pedro, iboga etc. are useful for expanding the level of awareness of humans. You can increase your temporary level of consciousness with all your drugs. The use of mind-altering drugs can enhance a person's creativity or mental abilities by connecting the person with a higher intelligence for a moment. The use of mind altering drugs can make a person temporarily creative. Both drugs that come from natural plants and chemical pills are medications. You can expand your consciousness with synthetic substances, not just those that are plant based.

The ingestion of DMT can cause meaningless hallucinations and it can also help in making connections with higher intelligence. There are certain groups that use it in Africa. Some of you think marijuana does the same. Sometimes it can take you to meaningful connections with higher intelligence and sometimes it is meaningless hallucinations.

There are certain types of coffee that you should avoid and there are some that are okay. You can drink coffee that was not supplemented with other liquids. Coffee can be very healthy because it stimulates the arteries.

Starbucks coffee contains nicotine. That is why people need their fix in the morning. Be careful not to overdose. Only have a little drink now and then. Nicotine is fine to open up the arteries. Sometimes it is made positive. It is a drug that is positive. Forget about decaffeinated coffee.

If a person uses a lot of artificial sugar in his diet, there could be an increased likelihood that the person will develop cancer. It depends on the health of the person whether much artificial sugar will lead to cancer. Sugar substitutes such as Sweet & Lo are not harmful to your health if you don't overdo it.

Only a few foods are harmful when not consumed in abundance. In some conditions artificial sugar is not helpful. If a person has bad teeth, it is not going to make the teeth any better. If a person has bad teeth, it is preferable to use artificial sugar.

A pill called Prevagen which is widely advertised as being helpful to aid a person's memory is effective for some people, but detrimental or ineffective for others.

In some cases the fluoride that has been added to your drinking water is harmful to your health but usually it is not. Food heated in plastic containers is more harmful to people. It causes increased deterioration of your foods.

## Healing devises and external aids

Any object whatsoever that a person believes to have healing qualities will be effective in healing if he believes so, no matter how nonsensical it may be.

Scalar energy is an effective healing modality that has to be looked into. It will be used much more extensively in the future.

The wearing of a battery powered wrist watch can be of healing benefit in some cases. The same true of magnets. Sometimes it is true that magnets will bring anything to the person. It depends on both the magnet and the person.

There is no truth to the theory that, because of modern technology, humans are being excessively bombarded with positive ions and this is having a negative effect on their health. Devices that produce or are imbued with negative ions are not of benefit to our health. Such devices are not of importance.

The wearing of gold can be of benefit to the health of the human physical body.

Much of what is said about various kinds of crystals being able to aid humans or to bring healing is correct; when one's soul wishes it to be of assistance, when one believes that this will be it will be.

The use of castor oil packs for health reasons as described by Edgar Cayce will be effective.

It is therapeutic for people to be in the ocean water.

Using a laser beam on water or food before it is consumed can be more beneficial to a person's health than if the laser beam had not been used. The same is true of using a laser beam on the meridian lines of the body to promote healing.

In the 1930's Wilhelm Reich invented the Orgone Box. That device could actually have some healing effect on those inside of it, especially if they believed it.

The Quantron Resonance System is a very valuable and effective healing modality.

Sitting in a salt room will help improve some health problems. It will be very successful and even for animals.

**Protection**

A person can endow any object to serve as an effective good luck charm or an object of protection if they believe in it. If you think that something is a lucky charm for you, it can become so. It can actually be effective if you feel that way. You are limiting your potential if you do not believe in good luck charms.

Physical objects such as a statue of St. Jude placed on the dashboard of your car or a mezuzah placed at the doorway of your home or amulets are not imbued with special powers, such as for protection or healing. However, they will bring protection, healing and comfort to those who believe.

Water can dissolve negativity that is potentially harmful to humans. Water is water. It is not holy. It is no more effective if it has been blessed by a priest than if from out of the faucet. Placing a glass of water on your nightstand will help keep negative energy away. Do not use if for nurturing yourself. It will keep evil spirits away as they are fearful of water

Making the sign of the cross with your hand in front of your chest as done by the Catholics does not actually bring assistance or protection to the individual doing so but it does give you peace of mind.

You can protect yourselves from negative energies. Don't think negative. Don't let negativity enter our mind. Change your negatives to positives.

## Visualization and channeling energy

Visualize surrounding someone with white light can be of actual benefit to that person. White light is beneficial to all people.

A person can send healing energy to another person merely by his thoughts.

If you are weak and cannot resist the flow of negative energy, it is possible to take on someone else's disease or problem when you are channeling healing energy to them.

Healing energy can be passed on from one person to another when one person touches another person but the healing energy that is transferred will be increased if more than one person at the same time touches the person who needs healing.

If a person visualizes that he is physically exercising, rather than actually performing physical exercises, that could have a positive effect on the physical body. Of course actual physical exercise is always preferable when possible.

Humans can definitely remove physical pain from their body by treating the pain as if it were a conscious entity. They should tell it to leave and also visualize it going away.

**Diseases: diagnoses, causes and cures**

There are known cures for various types of cancer but our government is creating a cover-up. There has been research where they are curing cancer with viruses like measles and cold viruses. In a way, these therapies are going to become cures.

Physical ailments are frequently the result of emotional disorders. Many of them, such as a headache or ulcers, are caused by stress.

People sometimes make the choice at the soul level to have a particular disease or physical problem so that they can advance more rapidly in their spiritual evolution.

If you wish for a long painful death at the subconscious level, such as from cancer, that can help alleviate karmic debts.

The cause of the 2014 Ebola virus outbreak was a natural occurrence, not manmade.

The sounds made by a person speaking will indicate specific health problems he might have. That technology is available now.

When we have an illness, we must understand that the illness is only the tip of the iceberg. The source of the problem is that we are not taking our life in the right direction. We can stop ourselves from having serious illnesses by understanding that something is wrong in our life and by changing it. We can do it by changing our thinking, our attitudes and our actions. The material written by Louise Hay is pertinent.

The Zika mosquito can be used in some manner for the improvement of a person's health, such as stopping the growth of cancer. It will be found to be able to halt any more growth of tumors. The injections will be made and they will be made to be a positive use.

What appears as defects, such as blindness or deformed body, has been intentionally created by those conscious entities responsible for the construction, growth and maintenance of our physical bodies rather than such conditions occurring just by random chance. There is no such thing as random chance. It is a learning ability. If a person is born with some kind of defect whatsoever that was intentionally done in the creation of that person's physical form.

A cleansing of the body or elimination of toxins will help cure sleep apnea. Throat exercises are also an approach to cure obstructive sleep apnea. Sleep apnea is caused by an overactive mind.

Throat exercises and eliminations of poisons in your system are both important to your system. Concentrate on what you are doing, one thing at a time not two, three or five things.

There is a complete breakthrough for Alzheimer's in existence but it is not publicized. It was derived in another country but it can be used in our country. Alzheimer's can be detected through the investigation of our DNA. If we were to examine a person's DNA, that could be used to predict the onset or possible onset of Alzheimer's.

It is possible that a person's DNA can be altered so the person will permanently be prevented from having specific diseases such as cancer, Alzheimer's, Parkinson's etc. It can be altered but it is not being altered at this time. There is no knowledge of them being able to do this before birth but they will do it after birth. Humans will do that on a regular basis, not just experimentally.

Stem cell implants are a healing modality that is worthy of continued injections and further research. Implants are very worthy when given the correct stem cells. They are experimenting with animal stem cells for humans. Rather than rabbits, pigs would be better. They are more like humans than other animals.

Schizophrenia is related to the malfunctioning of the pineal gland. This gland is what you call the third eye. The interior of the third eye is similar to the interior of the other two eyes. One of the symptoms of schizophrenia is that people often hear voices in their heads that others do not but you cannot assume that the cause of schizophrenia is the influence of negative non-physical entities.

HIV was a virus engineered by humans. It was done to reduce the earth's population of homosexuals.

Cancer can be cured by pumping more light into your DNA. Eating a few apricot pits a day can increase the light in your DNA, like walnuts would. It is ridiculous that drinking water that has been stored in a pyramid can do that also.

There is a relationship between chicken pox and multiple sclerosis. Chicken pox can make a person more susceptible to or lead to multiple sclerosis.

Humans are prone to certain physical problems because of extraterrestrials having tampered with their DNA. Many extraterrestrial groups have spliced their DNA with human DNA but this is not a negative action for humans.

## Miscellaneous

There are times that organ transplants and blood transfusions can affect the recipient in more ways other than just on the physical body. This can occur on the emotional and mental levels at times. When the recipients are sensitive, they can pick up the memories of the donor since memories are stored in the cells of the body. They can also pick up emotions.

The intentional provocation of an out-of-body experience could be detrimental to an individual's physical health if they do not protect themselves.

Living near high tension electrical lines or a radio transmitting tower can affect a person's health. It can also claim more energy from a person's psychic or medium abilities. It can decrease their ability as well as increase it.

The use of cell phones that so many of us carry can interfere with our sensitivity. It is not good for us to have as much electromagnetic radiation radio waves going through our bodies all the time. Cell phones can indeed affect our health.

Saying "I want to stay well." is much stronger than saying "I don't want to get sick." In other words, when we pray or when we think or visualize something, we should think in the positive, not the negative. The positive is heard. The negative is not heard. When you say "I don't want to get sick." "I want to get sick." is heard.

Although it appears that there is an increase in the incidence of neurological diseases, it is not an increase but we are just becoming more aware of it.

People are now living to be in their nineties and more than one hundred years old. The causes for that have been a change in diet, a change in health care and a change in lifestyle.

Humans will be able to survive if a pig's heart is transplanted into them. Pigs are very much like other animals that are on Earth. You don't necessarily need a human heart donor. It is possible to transplant a pig's heart into a human.

When a person is what we might say "out of their mind" and, for example, screaming that there are hundreds of bugs crawling all over their body when that is obviously not true for those with that are with him, it is preferable to tell the person that there are no bugs. It is not better to go along with the hallucination.

Honesty and complete truth will always be best. The truth is very important. Even though it may welcome a fight or argument between the two, it is better to tell the truth rather than to try to be nice and go along with them.

The Chinese meridian lines on the body that show the body's parts have been accurate for thousands of years and they have been helpful in many, many ways. You don't have to use only acupuncture needles but pressure points also help.

Children who grow up playing in dirt and with animals and who are not overly protected from germs develop a stronger immune system than children who grow up in a more sterile and protected environment. It depends on the immune system of the child. Sometimes a child can be overly protected.

# INSECTS AND ANIMALS

## Evolution of animals

Extraterrestrials have influenced the development of mankind and they also have had an influence on the creation or the development of insects and animals on Earth.

All species of animals can incarnate directly into the human kingdom. There is no chain of evolution among the animals. Animals can incarnate in a variety of species before evolving into a human. Some do but some can repeatedly reincarnate in just one species and then evolve into the human kingdom.

Animals are much more sensitive than humans. They are very psychic and know ahead of time when things are going to happen. They know when it is going to rain before it rains. When animals are about to cross over to the spirit world, they are aware of that. Animals are sensitive to the thoughts and emotions of people. They are very sensitive and can smell you from a great distance.

At times animals have soul groups, much the same as humans do.

Karma plays a role in their world.

The level of consciousness of whales and dolphins is closer to that of humans than to the level of consciousness of other animals.

Insects in their evolutionary journey can eventually evolve into angels. They do not evolve into animals or birds. Birds and any kind of insect can evolve into angels. They do not evolve into elementals but animals do so.

Animals, including insects, fish and birds cannot exist that are not part of a complete soul. Each animal belongs to a soul; even insects, even ants. All forms of physical manifestations are part of a soul, any kind of soul.

## Animals and reincarnation

Animals reach a point where they incarnate as humans. Certain kinds of animals are not more likely to reincarnate as humans than other kinds. Humans first incarnate as animals before incarnating as a human but it is not possible for a human to reincarnate as an animal. There are some animals that are better than some humans.

Domestic animals are more likely to reincarnate as humans. They have bonded with their human masters and are more likely to reincarnate as a human than are wild animals. When a person has a pet they are very attached to and the pet almost acts as if it were partly human, that animal is likely to reincarnate as a human. Humans can help in the evolution of animals by having them as pets.

Animals reincarnate differently from humans. A cat won't always reincarnate as a cat but a human will always reincarnate as a human.

Humans and spirits can have memories or emotions that developed from the time when they were incarnated as animals Fears such as fire or drowning can transfer from the animal to the human or spirit.

Animals reincarnate the same as humans and can live in parallel lives; that is, lead many lives simultaneously.

There are times that domestic animals are predetermined to be with their owners. Some owners are like parents but sometimes pets do not wish to be like their children.

If animals are part of species that becomes extinct, they will reincarnate in a different species. When animals reincarnate, they don't always reincarnate in the same species.

Animals have the same type of karma that people have, not like a group-type of karma.

Animal totems that are said to hover over each person's head are a reality. They are part of a composition, a build-up of strength to help the individual gain strength.

It is a human decision whether or not mankind should endeavor to protect endangered animal species whose endangerment is not caused by mankind.

In 80 years the majority of humans will no longer eat the flesh of animals but it will take many centuries before all humans cease to eat animal flesh.

Sometimes it is true that apes are the errant genetic descendants of humans rather than the reverse.

We should talk to our pets and tell them how much love and care for them. They will hear us and understand us.

When an entity reincarnates from the animal kingdom to the human kingdom, the species of the animal can have an effect on the personality of the new human but will have very little effect on the physical aspects.

Spirits can communicate with animals in the physical world as well as with animals in the spirit realm. They can also Influence animals' thoughts.

Animals in the spirit realm can show themselves to humans much the same as do the spirits.

Since entities in the spirit world can create what they want with their mind, it is possible to create one of the person's animal pets when they were incarnated.

**Non-human creatures**

The grotesque beings, part subhuman and part animal with weird appendages that Edgar Cayce described actually existed and they still exist. They are part human and part animal and act in animalistic ways. They are what Cayce referred to as the "things". They came into existence through natural development, not through genetic manipulation.

Creatures of extraterrestrial origin exist on Earth today. The huge human-like footprints found in the Himalayas were made by one of the creatures that we call Bigfoot or Sasquatch that are seen throughout the world They have a brain and some of the abilities that humans have and also some abilities that humans don't have. They are mystical beings and have been around for ages and they continue to propagate.

Some of the strange creatures that have been reported seen throughout the centuries are not the offspring of a human and an extraterrestrial, but some are.

Mermaids are real and they still exist. They are beings that had the upper part of a woman and the lower part of a fish. There is a basis for the legends about vampires. Blood sucking humans existed in the past and they still exist today.

There are creatures in the sea that are larger than the largest mammals, larger than any land mammal or any whale or octopus. The underwater beings we refer to as Telchines actually exist.

A monster exists in the waters of Lake Champlain that is the size of people. That creature is related to the Loch Ness monster but the Loch Ness monster has passed on.

**Miscellaneous**

Animals have intuition as well as instinct.

Animals can be possessed by evil spirits and they can be earthbound and not cross over.

There is what we might call a "mystical" connection to the scarab beetles portrayed in ancient Egyptian beliefs or drawings. The ancient Egyptians grew them and revered these beetles.

There is factual historical significance in the American Indian mythologies which often portray beings that are part ants and part humans that still exist on Earth.

In recent years, extraterrestrials were the cause of the numerous mutilizations of animals across America in which certain organs had been surgically removed for experimental reasons and for research.

Memories in animals can be passed on through the genes from one generation to the next. The same is true for humans. Memories of our ancestors could cause us confusion.

Animals have free will and when love is expressed by the human the animal will respond with love.

We should not feel guilty about animals that we had euthanized when they were suffering greatly because they are then happy to be free and relieved.

Although dragons play a prominent role in Chinese drawings they do not exist. What the Chinese depicted in their ancient drawings as dragons were actually spaceships. There was no animal involved as dragons but that is how the Chinese interpreted what they saw in the sky.

There are animals on other planets whose physical bodies were modified by DNA injections by extraterrestrials.

# JESUS, ISLAM, AND THE BUDDHA

Jesus is an extremely highly evolved human. His high level of evolution enabled a master spirit to share his body with him and thus Jesus became a split soul. There are 73 masters who are in charge of the spirit world. They are at the highest possible level of any entity on the spirit realm. Both Jesus' spirit and the master's spirit were in the same body for the final three years of his life.

Jesus the man was a highly evolved soul but not a Christ until the last three years or so of his life. Many of the words of Jesus were words of Jesus the Christ, such as when he said "I and my father are one."

Jesus was predestined to assist in the elevation of humanity. This enabled him to be a Christ; not a Christ like the millions of Christs that have preceded him or come after him, but rather one of the highest level Christs in the history of mankind.

Christs are highly evolved souls who incarnate for the purpose of helping and elevating the consciousness of mankind. There have been many Christs throughout history and more than ten thousand are incarnate on Earth today. Jesus spent most of his lifetime preparing to be a Christ but it was not intentional. He did not want to be of the status that he later became in life.

Jesus was a very different kind of man than what is portrayed by religion; not with blond hair or blue eyes but he was black with curly hair. What is written about Jesus is closer to reality as portrayed in the Koran than it is in the Bible. His name was pronounced Yaho in the Aramaic language.

Joseph was not Jesus' birth father but he did have nine children of his own. He had a great influence on the upbringing of Jesus, taking him many places throughout the known world at that time; Egypt, Persia or India for the purpose his education.

Jesus was what could be called a psychic and he was also a medium but his feelings were more to what you call psychic as he could see the future of people who could get well.

Jesus was a powerful healer who loved and cared for people and loved helping them.

Jesus actually physically died at the crucifixion and was aware of what was about to happen and was not ready to argue or fight. He was under restraint and overrun by his enemies and also his friends. He voluntarily incarnated knowing that he would serve as a Christ and be crucified.

Jesus now dwells in the spirit world but the Christ spirit has withdrawn. Jesus is a very gentle man in the spirit world and is shocked at what is happening on Earth with his name and had no idea he would be worshipped like this.

Both Jesus the man and Jesus the Christ performed miracles. A lot of the information in the Bible about the miracles is imaginary. He healed the sick and cast out demons but he did not raise the dead. He did not change water into wine nor did he calm the stormy sea. Although exaggerated, he did feed many people with just a few loaves of bread and two fish. His catching a fish with a gold coin in its mouth is just a story. Jesus did not perform all of the miracles attributed to him but Jesus the Christ did perform many miracles and gave others a great amount of happiness and security.

He had a good sense of humor and enjoyed life. He was married to Mary Magdalene and was the father of her children.

Jesus and an increasing number of children born today, that we call star children, can do things that far exceed the abilities of others.

Although Jesus was not a Christian but a Jew, you do not have to be either for Jesus to answer your prayers.

Jesus is a very powerful spirit whose work is helping people and whenever you call him, he is there for you. He continues to heal and bring comfort to people on Earth. There are other spirits who can help people as he does.

Jesus is going to make a second coming as said in the Bible; that is the personality Jesus will reincarnate and walk among us. He and Moses will appear at the same time.

A good deal of the information about the birth of Jesus in the Bible is more fiction than fact. Although there were palm trees in the desert, Palm Sunday did not exist nor was he born with Christmas trees around him. December 25 was not the actual date of Jesus' birth. He was not born in a stable and they weren't riding on donkeys. Joseph was quite a wealthy man and Jesus was born in a luxurious home. He was in a comfortable family and Joseph loved his son and all his children. He was a good father to all.

Both Joseph and Mary had considerable influence on Jesus. Joseph went with Jesus to many places to study while Mary was busy with the children and keeping a kosher household. Mary was Jesus' mother but Joseph was not his natural father.

Joseph married Mary in order to protect her. It was considered to be a virgin birth because Mary became pregnant by the rubbing of her body with that of a man without penetration.

When Jesus arose from the grave, as the Christian scriptures say, and people saw him, they saw what they wanted to see. The plasma, the ethereal body, rising from his physical body could be seen.

The shroud of Turin was used to cover his body and was very uncomfortable and annoying.

There is some truth in what Tom Harpur says about the Pagan roots of Christianity such as the details about Jesus birth, miracles and crucifixion. They were based on ancient Egyptian traditions. The account of Jesus as being born of a virgin is modeled after older traditions.

There is a special bond between Jesus and the archangel Michael; the choices and love that they have very deep within themselves. Jesus was not an incarnation of the Archangel Michael. The archangel Michael played a significant role in the ministry of Jesus and at times Michael influenced Jesus' thinking.

There was a soul connection between Jesus and his cousin John the Baptist but they are two different entities. John was considered to be a trouble maker.

Jesus' disciples continue to do healing from the other side as Jesus does now but there is no comparison to the work that Jesus does.

More highly evolved souls in the spirit world have a greater amount of energy than less evolved souls and they can be of greater assistance to humans. Jesus is called most often and he has the energy for that.

If you say "Help me Jesus." it brings on the assistance. It also brings assistance if you call on Mohammad or any other name. There are others in the spirit world whose stature is similar to that of Jesus.

Jesus channels information to many humans and frequently appears to them in dreams.

Scriptures say that he was the only begotten son of God but we are all begotten sons of God.

As a highly evolved soul, Jesus dwells in both the spirit world and has six multiple simultaneous incarnations on Earth at the present time. They are incarnations of the soul but not of the personality Jesus.

As many Christians believe, it is true that Jesus will be there to greet them when they cross over if they very strongly wish so.

There is some truth in his book *Lives of the Master* in which Glen Sanderfur talks about the previous incarnations that Jesus had according to Edgar Cayce.

When a fire broke out in Notre Dame Cathedral in Paris, an item called the Crown of Thorns was rescued but it was not actually the crown of thorns that was placed on the head of Jesus at the time of his crucifixion.

The Buddha is the highest level spirit in the astral world. His name is not Buddha but it is simply a title meaning the wise one that his followers have given him. He is a humble, gentle, modest soul who does not want to be worshipped.

He does not claim to be God or anything other than what he is. He is an energy being who is more powerful than any other spirit;

that is, he has more energy than any other spirit. He has more than sufficient energy to answer anyone's prayers regardless of their religion.

He does not like religion because religion is manmade and was not created by God. His energy is endless and cannot be drained. When in your best interest he can answer your prayers immediately. He will not answer your prayers if they are not in your best interest. He will not answer your prayers if they interfere with your karma or your freewill or with the karma or freewill of other people.

He does not want you to kneel down or perform any kind of ritual when you pray. If you did so, that would be worshipping him. Just think or, if you prefer, just say your prayer out loud. If you pray for healing, he can heal you or others if it is in your or their best interest.

You can pray for the healing of others as well. If you so wish, he will be there to greet you when you cross over to the spirit world. He assists those in the spirit world as well as those in the physical world. He works in conjunction with other spirits such as Jesus.

Over the millennia he has had 487 incarnations. He was always a very ordinary looking person, sometimes a male and sometimes a female, not at all with the appearance as he is depicted by his followers. He does not like the chubby statues of his image, or any other images that are made of him. He wants to be thought of as just an average looking man or woman.

His most recent incarnation was 4454 plus 2021 years ago. He has had many multiple simultaneous incarnations. His first incarnation was 40,542 years ago. His most recent incarnation was in what is now India. He has had had 11 incarnations after the Great Flood. They were in what are now China, Japan, Korea, Vietnam, Cambodia, Laos, Tibet, Iran, Pakistan, and Bangladesh as well as in India.

He was not only Indian or oriental in appearance, but in various incarnations he was also black, white, red, and Polynesian. Do not think of him as of any particular race.

Before the Great Flood he had incarnations on Atlantis, Lemuria and other long lost continents as well as incarnations on or in other planets or moons. Although he abides in the spirit world of the earth, his home planet was not Earth. His first incarnation was in the Pleiades.

Although Moslems do not believe in reincarnation, the following information about the previous lifetimes of Muhammad was received. He has had had 384 incarnations. He was not always a male but often a female.

He has reincarnated since the time of Muhammad. His most recent incarnation began in the year 1718. He has had many multiple simultaneous incarnations.

His first incarnation was 21,510 years ago. His most recent incarnation was in Saudi Arabia.

He has had had nine incarnations after the Great Flood. They were all in the Middle East and he was Middle Eastern in appearance in all nine incarnations.

Before the Great Flood he had incarnations on Atlantis, Lemuria and other long lost continents as well as incarnations on or in other planets or moons. He abides in the spirit world of the earth. His home planet is Earth.

The following statements regarding Islam are taken from various sources to highlight some of the basic beliefs; but not practices, history, achievements etc. of the religion.

God is one and Indivisible; He has never had offspring, nor was He born. There is none comparable to Him. No human eyes can see God till the Day of Judgment.

The creation of everything in the universe was brought into being by God's command as expressed by the wording, "Be, and it is", and that the purpose of existence is to worship God without associating partners to Him.

God is not a part of the Christian Trinity. He is viewed as a personal god who responds whenever a person in need or distress calls him.

There are no intermediaries, such as clergy, to contact God. God does not have human form.

Angels are fundamental to Islam. Duties assigned to angels include, for example, communicating revelations from God, glorifying God, recording every person's actions and taking a person's soul at the time of death.

Angeles are often represented in anthropomorphic forms combined with supernatural images, such as wings, being of great size or wearing heavenly articles. Angels are God's messengers with wings—two, three, or four common characteristics for angels are their missing needs for bodily desires, such as eating and drinking.

Their lack of affinity to material desires is also expressed by their creation from light: angels of mercy are created from 'light' in opposition to the angels of punishment created from 'fire' Muslims do not generally share the perceptions of angelic pictorial depictions, such as those found in Western art.

Prophets are human and not divine, though some can perform miracles to prove their claim. Besides prophets, saints possess blessings and can perform miracles.

Saints rank lower than prophets and they do not intercede for people on the Day of Judgment. People would seek the advice of a saint in their quest for spiritual fulfillment.

The time of the resurrection is preordained by God but unknown to man. All humankind will be judged by their good and bad deeds and consigned to paradise or hell. God will forgive the sins of those who repent if He wishes. Good deeds, like charity, prayer, and compassion towards animals, will be rewarded with entry to heaven. Heaven is a place of joy and blessings.

Every matter, good or bad, has been decreed by God and is in line with destiny. Nothing occurs outside of His divine decree: Nothing will ever befall us except what God has destined for us.

# KARMA

When most of us think of karma the first thing that usually comes into mind is paying back for the wrongs we have done but karma is much more than that. It is simply a case of cause and effect, even if we think of karma as being either negative or positive. Karma is not judgmental but rather simply the reaction for every action that is taken. All actions, thoughts and spoken words have consequences.

There is no difference between what we think of as positive karma and what we think of as negative karma. Karma is just karma, an element needed for the evolution of the soul.

People do not bring all aspects of their karma into each incarnation, only those that are to be focused on in that particular incarnation. Before reincarnating a person does not have a choice regarding which aspects of his karma should be avoided in the new lifetime.

You do not continue to bring the same aspects of your karma into each incarnation until that aspect is completed. What you consider to be negative karma cannot be released without bringing it to completion.

There are highly evolved entities that we call the Lords of Karma. They determine which aspects of a person's karma should be involved in each reincarnation. A spirit does not choose which aspects of karma should be addressed in the reincarnations.

Karma is what your future is to be. There is nothing threatening or anything to be afraid of in regard to karma. It is the dealing of cards; which hand you are given and how you play your hand of cards.

Karma exists at all levels of evolution. It does not begin when the soul is just a consciousness but rather when it manifests itself in the mineral kingdom. Minerals, vegetables, animals as well as humans and extraterrestrials have karma. Nature spirits as well as celestial bodies including planets and stars have karma. Karma exists at all levels of evolution and is an unending necessity for all souls.

Karma does not relate only to the physical world but also some aspects of karma can be played out in the astral realm as well as in the realms above that. Spirits can learn and grow just as much as in our world. Karma plays a role in the spirit world.

In the spirit realm an individual can still have what some of us might refer to as karmic debts and still have much to learn and yet not be required to ever reincarnate. A Christ spirit is not necessarily perfect in all aspects.

In no circumstances can individuals be absolved of paying back what we might think of as karmic debts in order that the slate is swept clean, so to speak. There is no way of getting around it because what some call a state of grace where karma is balanced does not exist. Karma cannot be absolved by anyone else, whether by humans, spirits or any other kind of entity.

It is not possible for an advanced soul to remove someone's negative karma but they can help remove it by forgiving. It is possible to assume the karmic debts of another entity.

A person's will power can be so strong that it can be used to override or negate the effects of predetermined karma in a lifetime. Even if something is predetermined, it can be changed by the exercise of free will.

When in the spirit world, there is a point where individuals become aware of the karmic cause of why seemingly negative things occurred to them while in the physical. At that time they will be able to make the connection between things that seemed negative and their karmic cause. We will understand that we are not being punished.

Karma is not affected differently if a person commits any kind of wrong and is punished while in the physical than if he had not been punished.

People are sometimes confronted with what are perceived as problems or negative situations that are not the result of their karma but are instead learning opportunities presented to the individual.

Spirits are aware of the karma of individuals in the physical dimension, even though we may not be aware of our own karma.

The language a person speaks can influence or reflect his character, personality or karma in the spirit world.

Minerals, vegetables and some groups, especially like nations or other large groups of people, have group karma. Animals do not have group karma.

Natural weather disasters are sometimes the reaction of karma but that has not been the case with the island of Haiti. Karma does not play a role in the numerous natural disasters that have affected that country.

It was the karma of many of those in the black race to become slaves and so it was with the Jewish people.

The United States is now experiencing negative national karma payback because of its history with slavery.

Karma has a domino effect and is a process that never ends.

An individual is not held accountable in a karmic sense for the actions of his ancestors unless he is the reincarnation of the ancestor. Each individual is responsible for himself because each has his own individual will.

Sometimes a person can wish at the subconscious level for a long painful death to help resolve karma.

When people are born blind or in some way physically defective, it is not always the result of karma nor is it the result of mistakes by the intelligent entities that created him. It can be an opportunity to teach them to learn and grow faster.

When a person is born malformed, conjoined or crippled in some way and then doctors are able to fix the problem, the doctors have absolutely not interfered with his karma.

If someone wrongs you or behaves evilly in this life, they will be eventually punished or get their "just desserts". The Bible says "Vengeance is mine sayeth the Lord". That is simply a reference to karma.

There is no such a thing as harmless lies that appear to have absolutely no consequences in a person's lifetime or future lifetimes. If a person repeatedly tells many lies about himself that have no negative impact on other people, those lies do have a negative impact on his own karma.

If you just don't know any better, you will still have to pay back for your actions. If you bring harm to others because of your ignorance, your karma is affected differently than if you were knowledgeable and intentionally caused them harm. Even though the results are the same your karma is different.

If you are a slow learner, you will eventually learn, often with the need for many reincarnations.

If a person is harmed by another person, the person that is harmed is done so because it is the result of his karma. They will be affected by whatever negativity they choose for someone else.

It is not always because of something you have done wrong in the past when you are what you perceive as being mistreated by someone, but rather an opportunity for growth.

If a person laughs when another person experiences physical injuries or suffering or misfortune, simply the act of laughing can create karma to cause the person who laughed to have similar misfortunes or suffering in a future lifetime. For example if they laugh when they see someone being hit by a car and the body is smashed, merely having laughed will affect their karma. They will have to pay some similar retribution in a future lifetime for having laughed.

Although many people feel that stealing something from another person is wrong but stealing from a large impersonal company such as large stores is less wrong, that is not correct. Since stealing is stealing, your karma is not affected differently.

Humans, spirits, elementals, as well as celestial bodies including planets and stars have karma.

# OTHER PLANETS AND THEIR INHABITANTS

## Other planets in the universe

All inhabited planets have one or more moons and atmosphere like that of Earth. All planets in other star systems which support human life have both climate and weather. They have several land masses surrounded by water which sometimes freezes and turns to ice.

There are planets which once had vegetation and animal life but no longer do so. There are also other planets and moons in our solar system that were once inhabited by humans. Most planets which do not have physical life have spirit life.

There are planets or moons in other star systems that support human life exactly as the earth does; light, air, temperature, nutrition, etc. There are planets that do not have humans or humanoid beings. Mars once had many features that are on the earth. There are humans beneath the surface of Mars right now.

There is such a thing as an intergalactic federation composed of various extraterrestrial groups. There are many extraterrestrial humans on Earth to help us to connect with extraterrestrials to the point that Earth may become part of the federation.

There are political land divisions on all other planets, such as the various countries of Earth. The mere fact that there are people on planets makes it so that there are political divisions.

All planets have some form of government, such as we have on Earth, with leaders, laws, politics etc.

Nineteen percent of the forty billion Earth-like planets in the Milky Way have human or humanoid inhabitants.

## Nature, climate, and land features

The land features of all other inhabited planets are similar to those on Earth; that is, there are mountains, valleys, deserts, jungles, rivers, oceans etc. All other planets have vegetation similar to that of Earth. The vegetation of Earth is comparable to that on other planets. They have fruits and vegetables very similar to those on Earth but they can vary. There are many different kinds of fruits and vegetables on different planets. Some of them have been brought to Earth by extraterrestrials.

Other planets have periodic cataclysms such as earthquakes, floods, tornados, hurricanes etc. as on Earth. It is the same as Earth as far as weather conditions. It rains and snows on other inhabited planets. There is a wide range of atmospheric temperatures on other planets as there is on Earth.

There many varieties of insects, birds, land animals and sea creatures on other planets. Some of those are the same as those on Earth. Every planet has life; different forms of life, insect life and animal life. To compare animal life to Earth is difficult because there are different animals on other planets. Every inhabited planet has something similar to human life.

Fire that the inhabitants can use exists on all other inhabited planets. Hydrogen and oxygen exist on all planets. Too much oxygen can be poisonous to both humans and humanoid everywhere.

## Physical aspects of inhabitants

There are entities on other planets that are the same as Earth people in appearance and there are still others who do not look like humans. There are others who are very different but have a humanoid form; a head, torso, arms, legs etc.

There are humans and humanoid beings on other planets whose physical bodies are not as dense as those of Earth people. They are more like the Lemurians in our history. In addition to having arms, legs, a head and a torso, there are extraterrestrial humanoids that have other visible human-like features such as skin, fingers, fingernails, toes and hair.

Some humanoids on other planets have different kinds of external coverings rather than human-type skin. Some are covered in leather, feathers or scales like reptiles. They do not all have hair. Quetzalcoatl, the god of the Aztecs, was covered with feathers rather than with skin.

There are alien races which are not human-like in appearance but rather more like insects, such as ants and praying mantises. The physical characteristics of humans of other planets do not provide any indication of their age as they do for Earth people.

Humans on all planets don't look any different from those who have recently incarnated. There are physical differences among the people of other planets in regard to their height, weight, skin color, and facial features as there are among Earth people. There is as much variety in the people of other planets as there is among Earth people. Both humans and humanoids have facial expressions that can reveal their emotions.

All planets have humans or humanoids of both male and female genders as well as bisexuals. Homosexuality exists on all planets. The reproductive process is designed to begin with a pleasurable experience as it is with Earth humans. It always requires two beings to reproduce. Although there are many individual exceptions, the need or desire to reproduce is implanted into the minds of individuals in all star systems.

The internal organs of the humans on all planets are the same as those of Earth humans. The appendix in Earth humans has been deactivated but on no other planet has it been deactivated. The deactivation of the appendix has caused the lifespan to be very much shorter than if had not been deactivated. The life span of humans on all other planets is considerably longer than that of Earth humans, often more than 30,000 years.

Human and humanoid inhabitants of other planets have the same five senses as do Earth humans.

## Non-physical aspects of inhabitants

The overall level of consciousness of Earthlings is lower than that of physical beings on other planets. Conversely, physical beings on other planets are at a higher level of consciousness.

All humans and humanoids in other star systems have attitudes and desires as part of their being. Inhabitants of other planets do not have the depth of emotions as that of Earth people. Their thinking is different.

People on other planets have a sense of humor. There is variation among the intellectual abilities of the inhabitants of all planets. Although they do not have the degree of emotions that Earth humans have, at times parents on most other planets have feelings of attachment to their offspring similar to that of humans.

Everything is individual but in some places they don't have the same feelings of attachments to their children. It is like you being attached to somebody's child.

The Grays reproduce exactly the same way as humans. They have done a lot of cloning over the millennia which has done damage to their DNA.

Humans and humanoids on planets in other star systems do not have the propensity for creating warfare as do Earth humans. On all other planets, humans and humanoids do not kill each other as earth humans do if they don't agree with one another. They are more advanced in their evolution because they do not kill the person who does not agree with them. Earth people are physically warlike but those on other planets are not physically warlike but still have the same arguing and disagreements.

Life is more peaceful in other systems than it is on Earth. People on other planets are sensitive to those around them. They appreciate the beauty of plant life and create beautiful gardens such as some of us do on Earth.

Inhabitants of other planets often keep animals in their homes but not as pets. They get close to certain animals as we do to dogs and cats. They use them for assistance similar to the way we use guide dogs

In all other star systems the inhabitants can create physical objects with just their minds, similar to the manner in which spirits create in the astral world.

The mineral, vegetable and animal kingdoms exist on all inhabited planets. Humans and humanoids evolve through the mineral, vegetable and animal kingdoms as they do on Earth. All humans and humanoids go through the animal stage before they evolve into a person.

There is as much dishonesty among extraterrestrials as there is among humans. Earth humans are not more dishonest than others.

Just as there are differences among the physical inhabitants of the various planets, there are also differences in the spirit worlds among the various planets.

## Extraterrestrial species

At the present time there are humans on other planets and moons in our solar system as well as various kinds of humanoids. The intent of the aliens that we call the Grays is that they wish to dominate, and they will. The Grays do not have as strong emotions as those of humans. They work only on facts. They do not cry like Earth humans cry or have the fear that the humans have.

On other planets as well as on Earth, humans and humanoids live above ground and underground. It depends on what area they are.

The density of population on other planets compared with the density of that on Earth is about the same.

Society has existed on other planets for what you might say hundreds of thousands of years more than Earth society.

Other planets are more pleasant places to incarnate than is Earth.

Money, or something similar, does not play an important role as it does on Earth.

Humans and humanoids in other star systems also have spirit guides as we have on Earth.

Although the ancient Sanskrit writings state that there are more than 400,000 humanoid species of extraterrestrials, the actual number is approximately 70,000. The number is decreasing because they are becoming humans.

Earth humans are not the only species in the universe whose physical bodies were created or modified by extraterrestrials. There are humanoid beings and animals on other planets whose physical bodies have been modified.

## Institutions and society

The concept of marriage does not exist on other planets. It is not a natural social institution, but rather the result of religious doctrine invented by man. Marriage is something that is an Earth feature rather than in other star systems.

The concept of family on other planets is attachment. It doesn't mean that you have to be born into, because we are born into the same race. Parents take part in the raising of their young but communal care of the offspring is more common on other planets. Our planet is gradually becoming so that the family unit will not be as important in the raising of the young as will be a communal environment.

Individuals on other planets have professions or special areas of work. They are waiting anxiously and happy to be called upon by us and wish to assist and aid those in pain.

Those on other planets are as attentive to the needs and care of their planet as are Earth people. Earth people at this moment should be more concerned about climate change but a lot of what is occurring is natural.

There are other planets where individuals do not need clothing or some kind of covering of the body because humanoids can be covered with feathers, scales etc. They don't have something comparable to our clothing but it is always nice to be adorned with body coverings.

On other planets the bodies of the dead are not buried in the ground, cremated, or cast into the sea. They just evaporate, turn to dust and dissolve because they make their bodies disintegrate just like the wind.

It is not necessarily of interest or a habit for people on other planets to record or preserve their history. They do not have things comparable to our history museums because they are not interested in their past or do they have museums that display works of art

Those on other planets treat each other more kindly and cooperate more with each other than do Earth people. They listen more and are not ones that think about their own situations when they communicate with each other as Earth people do.

Religions do not exist in any star systems in addition to ours. Religion is manmade.

Other star systems measure time based on their star, planets and moon as we do. They measure time on the rotation and revolution of their planet.

## Dwellings and buildings

The residential architecture on other planets is somewhat similar to ours. It varies a great deal among the different planets. Stone is very common in the materials used in their residences. Since wood decays, it is not used nearly as much elsewhere as it is on Earth.

Entities that inhabit other planets live both in what could be called metropolitan areas and in rural areas much the same as those on Earth. There are people that like to be in rural areas and lead lives that way much the same as we do.

On other planets dwellings are used as they are on Earth; that is, for individuals or families for both protection from the elements and privacy but not for protection from other people. Those shelters are usually manmade rather than natural. They are often beneath the surface of the planet, sometimes several stories deep.

The interiors of the dwellings on other planets do not necessarily have divisions used for specific purposes comparable to our rooms such as kitchens, bedrooms, recreation areas etc. Some extraterrestrials do have furnishings similar ours in their abodes if they are needed or if they wish that but they are not needed on all planets. Some humanoid beings on other planets can just live in nature without any thing of comfort. They can use nature more for their furnishings, and for beds they lie on the ground.

Some planets have buildings above ground that are many stories in height, higher than those on Earth.

Both public and private plumbing systems for obtaining water and disposal of sewerage on other planets are nothing compared to ours. Ours are far more elaborate.

## Communication and education

Those on all other planets do not need to communicate to each other through spoken language because they can easily use telepathy. When they use spoken language it is what we call Tongues; the same Tongues that people often speak in churches. The Earth is the only planet where you have to communicate with voice. All extraterrestrial groups can communicate with other extraterrestrials from other planets.

Those on other planets have learning centers where they can obtain knowledge but not as we have them. The young are not provided with what might be considered a formal school type of education as they are on Earth but they are educated by community members.

Those on other planets communicate with the angels, spirits and entities on other worlds the same as Earth humans can do.

## Nutrition and health

Vegetables are a necessary source of nourishment for human and humanoids on all inhabited planets in the universe.

Bodily diseases do not occur among the population of those on other planets. Diseases exist only on Earth. Individuals on other planets can be injured and need help to repair strength. The help comes from external sources but not necessarily just from within.

They do not have places where people can go to have their bodies repaired. They do not have medications but create their own resources which come from their own mental ability. There is no equivalent to medical doctors.

Agriculture is practiced on all other worlds to provide nutrition for their inhabitants. Inhabitants of other planets have farms that they create in order to feed the inhabitants and they also take things directly from nature without planning.

Nutrition on other planets is comparable to your putting gas in a car. Food is not food as we think of as food because they do not eat for taste as do Earth humans.

They consume vegetables that live in the sea and vegetables that grow on and in the earth. Humans and humanoids do not eat animal flesh even what comes from the sea. For people on all other planets, the intake of nutrition does not occur on a regularly scheduled basis as it does with Earth humans.

Those on other planets do not consume mind altering substances comparable to our alcohol and drugs.

The bodies of those on other planets need rest or sleep. Everyone needs rest but not necessarily sleep. Not everyone in the universe sleeps but many can rejuvenate themselves just by resting. Dreaming when asleep belongs more to humans than to extraterrestrials.

## Transportation and technology

In all other star systems humans and humanoids are more technologically advanced.

When humans or humanoids on other planets want to travel from one place to another, they do not need to use land vehicles on roadways comparable to our streets and highways. If they want to travel from one place to another they can fly in the air instead. They have vehicles like our ships that travel on the surface of the earth as well as vehicles that travel beneath the surface.

The wheel is an invention used for forms of transportation in all star systems. They have ground vehicles with and without wheels on other planets.

Electricity is a form of energy that is needed on all planets. Scalar energy is also a form of energy that is used throughout the universe.

Those on other planets measure such things as distance, weight, volume, energy etc. the same as Earth humans do.

On other planets nothing has to be artificial such as lighting, heating and cooling, or systems for the disposal of rubbish. Technologies such as air conditioning are not necessary. They simply create conditions for their likes and comfort with their minds.

Others worlds have means for reproducing sounds, sights and visual activities including sound recordings, still photography, and motion pictures. The measurement of time is important and therefore they have instruments such as clocks and calendars.

There are UFO's from other star systems large enough to transport thousands of people.

## Work, business and leisure

Individuals on other planets do not enjoy the visual arts such as painting and sculpture etc. The arts do not exist in the spirit worlds either. Music exists on all planets.

On other planets people do not need physical activities because their bodies do not need it. They do have physical activities for pleasure such as sports.

Private ownership does not exist on some other planets. They do not have the conditions we have on Earth but they are able to share ownership. They are more like the American Indians where there was no private ownership of land.

On other planets, there is no need for specific places that house the various kinds of materials or goods that individuals may need where they can obtain them. Everybody makes for themselves whatever they need.

Individuals on other planets have commerce of things that naturally occur on the planet. They can also communicate with those on all other planets.

Entities on other planets can do much more than Earth people can do because humans on Earth are the least advanced of any other planet. They do not have any limitations as we put upon ourselves on this planet.

Individuals on other planets travel for both work and pleasure; much the same as it is for Earth humans. We travel for work and we travel for pleasure and we travel for no reason at all. It is the same on all other planets.

Entertainment and activities for pleasure exists on all planets. Those on other planets enjoy playing mental games with each other more than do Earth people.

## Miscellaneous

Gold is an element that is treasured throughout the physical universe. Gold, silver and platinum are also treasured in other star systems. Extraterrestrials wish they had the ability to change other elements into gold but they are still trying.

Rare gems such as diamonds, emeralds and rubies are valued in other star systems but they do not put a dollar sign on them. Sometimes they make use of the less rare gemstones such as amethyst, quartz, and jade which are healthy and will bring on energy from different sources.

There are multiple births on other planets, like twins or triplets and also miscarriages. Some children die very young.

In other star systems, unlike on Earth, death not preceded by pain.

# PERSONALITIES

**The entries in this section are summaries of people who have been written about in other sections of this book.**

## In Biblical times

Adam and Eve were extraterrestrials who came to Earth in a space ship, the Garden of Eden, so that their descendants could intermarry with Earth people for the purpose of raising the consciousness of the population on Earth. They lived to be much older than Earth humans because their appendixes had not been deactivated as those of Earth humans had been done so by the Anunnaki.

The creator of Adam also created a wife named Lilith before Eve.

He had nine other wives simultaneously.

Noah was the last extraterrestrial descendant of Adam and Eve who, before the Great Flood, loaded the DNA of embryos of animals onto a space ship which rested on the crest of the waters until the rains stopped. The Earth was then repopulated by many people who were in the spaceship.

Lot's wife was pulverized in an atomic explosion as she was fleeing Sodom and Gomorrah.

Jonah was a prophet who was taken aboard a UFO that was resting atop the waters of the sea for three days.

Jesus was a very pious student from a wealthy family who became a split soul when the Christ spirit shared his body with him when he was 30 years old until he was 33 years old. During that time he was a Christ whom we refer to as Jesus the Christ.

John the Baptist was a cousin of Jesus who was considered a trouble maker because of what he was preaching.

Goliath was a ten foot tall Nephilim, the son of intermarriage between an Earth person and a giant from the planet Jupiter who came to Earth.

Aaron, the brother of Moses, was able to communicate with extraterrestrials and act as an intermediary between them and Earth people. He was not well liked by the Israelites.

Judas was portrayed as having betrayed Jesus in a way that would result in Jesus' crucifixion but he was greatly misunderstood and was a friend of Jesus whose role was predestined.

As a member of the royal family, there was a connection between Moses and King Akhenaton in ancient Egypt. He was the son of King Akhenaton and Queen Nefertiti. He was part extraterrestrial. It was because of the religious beliefs in one god and trying to change the religion of ancient Egypt that all traces of King Akhenaton and Queen Nefertiti were removed by the Egyptians after their deaths.

Jacob slept on a pillow that is thought to be The Stone of Scone that is now placed under the throne of the British monarchy, but it is not.

King Solomon had a ring that had supernatural powers which was provided by extraterrestrials.

## From the Biblical times to the 19th century

In the year 1139 an Irish priest, Saint Malachy Morgain, had a vision about the Catholic popes. He said there would be 112 more popes and made comments about them.

The magician Merlin as portrayed in the Arthurian legends of England did not exist.

The letter about Jesus supposedly written by Pontius Pilate to the Emperor Tiberius was a forgery written several centuries later.

Christopher Columbus was in search of a passage to the East but he was not interested in finding Atlantis. What he saw rising from the sea or was not a UFO but it was a natural phenomenon.

Leonardo DaVinci's painting of the Mona Lisa was a self portrait expressing himself in a feminine way with his smile. It is not a painting of an actual person.

Emperor Constantine IV of the Byzantine in the 7th century AD defeated the invaders by destroying more than one thousand ships with something called Greek fire which could not be extinguished with water. Although its formula was later lost and never rediscovered, it was actually oil.

Sir Francis Bacon, the illegitimate son of Queen Elizabeth I of England, actually wrote all of the works that Shakespeare dictated to him because Shakespeare didn't know how to write. Bacon could be considered as the father of Freemasonry.

George Washington received alien intelligence during the Revolutionary War that helped him with the war. He and the majority of the U.S. presidents were highly advanced souls.

## The 19th Century

Napoleon Bonaparte and Adolf Hitler were antichrists that Nostradamus predicted. There were, are and will be many more antichrists.

Abraham Lincoln was psychic and he received guidance from the spirit world through a medium. He wrote the Emancipation Proclamation himself. He was a Christ and the most hated president in our history; hated even more than President Trump. He is still in the spirit world and has not reincarnated because his work there is keeping him from reincarnating.

John Wilkes Booth assassinated President Lincoln but there were other people involved. President Andrew Johnson did not take part in the assassination. He was aware of the conspiracy to assassinate President Lincoln but did nothing to stop it.

Both Alexander Graham Bell and Elisha Gray invented the telephone but Bell received the patent and had more publicity.

In 1892 Lizzie Borden murdered her father and stepmother with an axe because she was both demented and very angry. She was treated badly and was avenging them.

## The 20th Century

Vice-President Lyndon Johnson disliked President Kennedy and was jealous of him because he himself wanted to be president. President Johnson knew the assassination was going to occur and he allowed it to happen. He was not directly involved. President Kennedy was predestined to be assassinated and President Johnson was playing a predetermined role. He was also indirectly involved with the assassination of Robert Kennedy.

There is some validity and accuracy in the books called *The Pyramid Power* and *The Pyramid Prophecies* written by Max Toth.

When Zachariah Sitchin interpreted the Sumerian tablets he was channeling his higher self but was discredited by scientists because he did not have the proper credits to make such proclamations. He was a highly evolved soul.

Elizabeth Kubler Ross was correct when she said that when a person's death is imminent, friends and relatives should not encourage that person to hold onto life but should give them permission to die.

Lee Harvey Oswald was recruited by a government official in the assassination of John Kennedy. He was not involved in recruiting Jack Ruby. Jack Ruby was honest, faithful and loyal but also stupid.

Amelia Earhart's plane crashed on land and provided food for cannibals in the jungle. It crashed because the oil in the machinery became dry and did not work well.

Princess Diana was accidently killed in the car because the driver was speeding and under the influence of legal medication and not enough sleep.

The death of the actress Natalie Wood was accidental when she slipped and fell and was not able to swim.

In 1949 Secretary of Defense Admiral Forrestal was murdered by the U.S. government because he had secret knowledge regarding Antarctica.

Admiral Byrd discovered advanced underground civilizations with people living underground at the South Pole. There was a cover-up by our government regarding his expedition to Antarctica after World War II.

Princess Grace Kelly of Monaco was killed in an automobile which her daughter was driving. It was an accident and it was hush-hushed that the daughter was driving. There was a rumor that the cause of the accident was that Grace Kelly had a stroke but the stroke was after the accident.

The murderer of Jean Benet Ramsey was an old man who had been imprisoned. He crawled through a basement window of their home and then went into the room of the child. He got into bed with her because she appeared as a young adult.

President Eisenhower and some of his advisors had face-to-face discussions with an extraterrestrial named Valiant Thor who said he was from Venus and who looked like a human.

O.J. Simpson murdered Nicole Brown and Ron Goldman without accomplices. He was under the influence of drugs during the time of the murder. He did not confess to anyone what he did, not even to himself. At the present time he wants to kill another person. He is a very angry, hostile person who is a fuse waiting to be ignited.

Saddam Hussein thought he was the reincarnation of King Nebuchadnezzar II but he was insane.

The Russian monk Rasputin was influenced by extraterrestrials and he was also simply deranged.

Michael Rockefeller in 1961 suffered a horrible death when his boat overturned of the coast of New Guinea.

The crash of the airplane in which John Kennedy Jr. was killed was an accident because he was blinded by the water. He was only thinking of himself. He was in an emotional state with his wife at that time.

In 1947 President Truman established a committee called the Majestic 12 to investigate extraterrestrial activities in the United States. The findings of that committee were very accurate.

Frederick Valentich and his plane disappeared while flying over water in Australia in 1978. They were abducted by a UFO. He survived physically but not mentally.

Zachariah Sitchin was correct when he said that some of the Anunnaki rulers lived to be more than 20,000 years as well as some who weren't rulers.

There is much truth in what Erich Von Daniken has written in his book *Chariots of the Gods.*

Dorothy Kilgallen was correct when she wrote newspaper articles about a crashed UFO in England in the 1950's.

The bandleader Glen Miller's airplane crashed in 1944 because it was ambushed. The plane has disintegrated and will never be found.

James Hoffa, the Teamsters Union leader, disappeared without a trace in 1971 because he was intentionally put into a tank that pulverized him so that his body couldn't be identified.

Mahatma Gandhi was visited by extraterrestrials that guided him and influenced his thinking.

President Reagan had face-to-face interaction with extraterrestrials and the assassination attempt on him occurred to prevent him from revealing information about extraterrestrials.

President Obama was born in the United States because Hawaii is part of the United States.

President John Kennedy betrayed the Illuminati by going against what they wanted and was assassinated because of the betrayal. The assassination was an event that was predestined.

The same is true of Robert Kennedy. He was assassinated as a convenience, just to get him out of the way.

Although it is rumored that Jimmy Carter was the half-brother of John Kennedy because they have very similar facial features it is not true.

The Clintons ran a cocaine business in Arkansas in the 1980's and 1990's. It was clandestine and related to the Iran Contra deal. It helped Iran a lot. They gave financial, industrial and military information to China for which they profited financially before Bill Clinton became president. Hilary Clinton is not well mentally and physically. She will not try for another nomination to be president but she will remain behind the scenes.

Vince Foster, who worked for the Clintons, committed suicide because he was going to testify against the Clintons and the pressure was too great.

In 1995 Timothy McVey bombed the Oklahoma City federal building because all the documents for the Whitewater investigation were there. His bomb was too small to create such a large explosion. It was a controlled demolition by the Cabal.

In the 1940's the actress Heddy Lamar was a very amazing lady who made inventions that made today's technology of WI-FI, GPS, Bluetooth and even the internet possible.

Marilyn Monroe died of an overdose of medication that she herself caused. The Kennedy family could not wait to get rid of her but they did not murder her.

During the Franco dictatorship in Spain, thousands of babies were stolen because their parents were opposed to Franco. Those babies were sold to other parents who supported Franco.

As Edgar Cayce has stated, a chamber under one of the paws of the sphinx called the Hall of Records contains a full account of the pre-history of mankind which will be discovered and exposed to mankind 107 years from now. The use of castor oil packs for health reasons as he described will be effective.

In the 1930's Wilhelm Reich invented a device called the Orgone Box that could have some healing effect on the person inside of it.

Edward Leedskalnin used sound to raise those heavy stones to build the Coral Castle in Homestead Florida.

Einstein used his psychic ability to develop the Theory of Relativity. His work was attributable to both his high IQ and assistance from extraterrestrials in developing that theory

The acceleration of the demise of religion to some extent can be attributed to the New Age movement that was purportedly begun by Helena Blavatsky and the Theosophical movement which followed. She channeled information from both spirits and angels.

Howard Hughes received information from extraterrestrials and his mental decline and demise was very much hastened by his enemies. He obtained the Tesla patents that were sequestered by the government.

George Van Tassel built a time machine that was confiscated by the government.

Nickola Tesla was a brilliant man who was assisted by extraterrestrial and many spirits. He created a UFO by discovering the key to overcome gravity. He also created what was called the death ray that caused of a huge explosion more than 1000 times more powerful than the atom bomb that took place in Tunguska Siberia in 1908. In 200 years we will transmit electricity wirelessly through the air on a large scale as Tesla tried to do.

## The 21st century

Saddam Hussein discovered a stargate which he was planning on using for nefarious purposes. He was a very controlling person. The Unites States invaded Iraq because we were aware that he had discovered a stargate.

Nikolas Cruz, the mass murderer of high school students, said that for years he was tortured by demon voices in his head that told him to kill. It is true that he heard such voices. He was deranged.

Both President Obama and President Trump were taken to see the civilization under the ice in Antarctica. They were threatened with extinction if they exposed this. Donald Trump established a Space Force because he had information about extraterrestrials there that the public does not know.

The main reasons that Supreme Court Justice Kavanaugh was so violently opposed by the Democrats were that he opposed abortion and that he was in favor of military tribunals for civilians accused of treason.

John McCain's career was not built on lies and deception as some people say. He did not broadcast anti-American propaganda to the Vietnamese people over the radio. He was a very loyal and kind man. John McCain was murdered by poison.

Anthony Scalia's death was not self-inflicted. He did not choose to go. He was murdered by opposing Democrat members in the House of Representatives because of his stance on issues they opposed.

Admiral Jeremy Boorda was murdered by government officials because he had information about extraterrestrials that they did not want him to reveal.

The cause of Robin William's suicide was an enemy whom he believed to be a friend.

John of God in Brazil raped more than 600 women. A person can actually do what we call miracles such as healing a person from disease and yet perform evil acts.

G. E. Kincade found artifacts in the caves in the walls of the Grand Canyon and then the Smithsonian Museum removed them and denied their existence.

In 2001 Donald Rumsfeld said that more than two trillion dollars from the Department of Defense could not be accounted for. That money was secretly used for our involvement in space.

Jesse Ventura is on the right path with his conspiracy theories. There is some basis or truth in most of the conspiracy theories that are circulating.

The leader in North Korea has a mishap in his brain. He is a man who is really in love with himself. He will last as a leader but he will not be very successful. Nothing is going to happen to the leadership in North Korea.

Russian president Putin is not a secret ally of the United States.

Teresa May, the former British prime minister, was justified in expelling Russian diplomats recently for that reason.

The information that David Wilcock provides about the Cabal and the Alliance is accurate. He possesses knowledge for which the Cabal would like to assassinate him. He is wise and his lifestyle and actions prohibit the Cabal from harming him. There are no plans to assassinate David Wilcock. He will not be assassinated. He is not of extraterrestrial origin. He is extremely honest and accurate in his findings. He is not an instrument of the Cabal but rather of the Alliance.

What Delores Cannon and Bob Olson say on You Tube is truthful and accurate.

Although Matt Gaetz is dishonest, he did not have physical relations with women against their will.

Rush Limbaugh was a highly advanced soul who was on target with his comments and could be referred to as a dear soul.

The current Delhi lama is not the reincarnation of the previous Delhi lama.

The information that Corey Goode presents on You Tube is worth our interest.

President Trump often needs less than two hours of sleep at night because more highly evolved humans need less sleep. He is a highly evolved soul although his ego personality may give a different impression. Through the use of his free will (i.e. his desires), Trump screwed up the predestined plans for him. He will lose influence on the Republican Party but the consequences of his actions as president will have a long lasting influence on our society

Hilary Clinton is a reincarnation of Jezebel and Bill is King Ahab.

Steve Jobs, the founder of Apple Computer, received information about his inventions from extraterrestrials and he took it with him when he left the physical world

## The 21st century in the future

Cuba's economy will be restored to a level of prosperity and the lifestyle of its citizens will be greatly elevated when the Castro regime ends with the departure of Raoul Castro. The government will become less socialized and more democratic.

Prince Charles will become the king of England for a very short time but he is a weakling.

Prince William, will absolutely be a good king and he will be king for a long period of time.

The Republican candidate will be Mike Pence. He will make the correct decisions as president. He will serve two terms as president. There will not be more political harmony between the two parties during Pence's presidency but there will be during the term of his successor.

Lady Gaga will change direction and seek to expose the Cabal and the harm they have done to her soul. It's like she sold her soul to the devil. She needed to be noticed. They promised her and they made her a star. She would not have got to the point where she is now if not for the Cabal. Selling your soul to the devil means allowing another entity or group to take over you.

Pope Francis will be the last pope as such but the Catholic Church will continue for some time. Two popes will head the papacy not just one as it has been in the past.

After the Ascension is completed in the year 11962.

Presidents Obama Biden and Reagan are highly advanced souls who will remain on Earth. All three had honest intentions.

Neither of the two Bush presidents had honest intentions nor will they remain on Earth.

Nancy Pelosi is a sincere person who will remain on Earth.

Chuck Schumer is not sincere and will not remain on Earth after the Ascension.

# REINCARNATION

Reincarnation is not what we have traditionally thought it to be. People are unique individual personalities. They appear as such for only one single lifetime. Reincarnation is when a soul manifests itself in a new physical body, not the entire soul but only selected personality aspects. The elements of the soul are the life force which animates it and the DNA of the soul. Within that DNA are the memories of all lifetimes, including all the knowledge attained in previous embodiments. The elements of the soul are present in the new body but not all the aspects of previous incarnations.

For the sake of a simplified explanation, we could compare the soul as a huge closet full of innumerable pieces of clothing of all types. Each piece of clothing is a specific aspect of the person-to-be. We are given a suitcase to pack to take with us for our new voyage. Obviously all the contents of the huge closet of clothes cannot fit into our suitcase. Only a few of the pieces of clothing will fit in the suitcase. Whatever is in our suitcase is all that we will need for the new incarnation.

There are occasions when the suitcase may have nearly all the same pieces of clothing as in the previous incarnation. In that case there is a strong possibility that even some of the same physical features will occur in the new incarnation. Memories of the previous incarnation could be retained, especially during childhood. Knowledge learned or abilities obtained in the previous incarnation could be readily accessed.

Even when the new suitcase does not contain nearly all the same pieces of clothing as in the previous incarnation, the inclusion of certain pieces of clothing could have the same effect as stated above

The author of this book has been informed that he is the reincarnation of both George Washington and Allan Kardec, the founder of spiritism. That is true only to a limited extent. It is simply that the three people are physical manifestations of the same soul. Apparently the piece of clothing for using the pendulum was in the suitcases of both George Washington and the author. Likewise, it appears that the piece of clothing for spirit communications was in both suitcases also. There are several additional parallels in the lives of Alan Kardec and the author.

Life in the physical is a necessary experience for all souls in the spirit realm. All spirits have to incarnate at least once. We all must suffer to be in the physical. When people do not learn, they must come back again.

There are entities in the spirit world that have never experienced life in the physical but most have. There are others who are now experiencing their first incarnation as a human. Some spirits do not need more incarnations and do not wish to reincarnate. They can remain where they are or they can move on to a higher level.

Before we reincarnate we select our parents and usually have had previous incarnations with them although there might have been a different combination of relationships. That choice is usually related to karma. Not just one parent but both parents are a significant factor in the choice. Before an incarnation the spirit of every newborn human baby is imbued with the language or dialect of its future parents

When to reincarnate is completely up to the decision of the individual but we do sometimes have a little push. The necessity for physical incarnations of Earth humans will never cease to exist. Reincarnation has always existed and will always exist. Humans cannot escape the reincarnation process but we can eventually reach a level of evolution where we are no longer required to reincarnate.

All spirits that have chosen to be part of the reincarnation cycle must remain in that cycle until they have reached a level that entitles them to forego future incarnations. Future incarnations are not available until they decide in which direction they should proceed. Spirits sometimes choose to reincarnate in order to help humanity after they have reached the status that reincarnation is no longer needed for them to reincarnate. They are called Christs.

After souls have crossed over to the spirit world they can reincarnate after a while or they can stay in the spirit world to rest before coming back. Souls can do whatever they are comfortable in doing and every individual soul is very different.

People have different lifetime experiences in all of the human races. There are absolutely no differences among the races.

With each incarnation a soul does not necessarily advance forward in its evolution. The current incarnation is not necessarily the most highly evolved.

Going back in history to reincarnate to a prior time is not possible.

People who die at a very young age are likely to reincarnate more rapidly than people who die when they are older. Miscarried children reincarnate. Problems are not caused in the spirit world when abortions are performed because spirits know in advance if an abortion will occur.

The great majority of people have no conscious recollections of their past lives even though many people seem to express curiosity about them. The loss of memory of previous lifetimes is built into the reincarnation process.

Most souls have a particular star system into which they prefer to incarnate and they tend to go back to the same star system because they are familiar and feel at home and safe there. When they retire from Earth, they can inhabit other planets in other forms.

Earth is the planet which provides the most difficult lifetimes on which to incarnate. It is the people on Earth that make it the most difficult planet for physical life. Earth humans are less evolved and less intelligent than the physical beings on other planets. The more advanced souls incarnate elsewhere rather than on Earth.

Souls have interplanetary sojourns for specific purposes in the spirit realm before they are able to reincarnate. Each planet in our solar system serves for a different purpose in the evolution of the soul. The earth's moon is a wonderful place for such decisions because there are so many options for a soul to select. There are specific lessons that the moon is noted for, just as the earth is needed for certain lessons.

Highly advanced entities that were once on Earth can eventually evolve to the state in which they can become a planet or a star. All the billions of stars out there are souls. Planets and stars have a level of consciousness that is far above the level of that of humans.

Spirits can choose to be knowledgeable about the physical world they are about to enter.

When people cross over to the spirit world they see what they want to see. Your spirit guide meets you just when you cross over and preferably family and loved ones are there also.

Attitudes, emotions and desires can change from one incarnation to another as a result of experiences in the spirit world between lifetimes.

Sometimes the knowledge you gain in a lifetime can be taken to the next lifetime.

Certain incarnation destinies are determined between lives and then the outcomes of those destinies are determined by the exercise of free will.

At times the length of a person's life is predetermined before birth but not cast in stone.

Before reincarnating a spirit sometimes makes the choice to have a particular disease or physical problem in order to advance more rapidly in its spiritual evolution.

The extent of an individual's ability to remember things increases somewhat from lifetime to lifetime as what we call déjà vu.

If a person becomes knowledgeable in a certain field of study in a lifetime, some of that knowledge can become easily retrievable in future lifetimes.

If a person is studious or observant and learns a lot while in the physical, that information will be somewhat retained when in the spirit form.

Gambling and other addictions could cause a predisposition for those same addictions in future lifetimes.

Birthmarks are often vestiges of fatal wounds in previous incarnations.

It is usually true that if people have severe mental or emotional disorders in a lifetime they are likely to have similar disorders in a future incarnation. Such disorders can be overcome in the spirit world before the future incarnation, but usually not.

Souls can reside in the spirit realm and simultaneously have several incarnations. They can have multiple simultaneous incarnations if they want to progress more rapidly. It is especially true when a new era on Earth is approaching such as the Ascension of our solar system. Souls can have incarnations on Earth and incarnations on other planets at the same time.

People who are part of a soul's multiple simultaneous incarnations may have friendly relations if they meet others who are also part of the multiple simultaneous incarnations or they may intensely dislike each other if they come into contact with one another. Sometimes it could be a split soul. Having a split soul can cause much confusion.

Before a spirit reincarnates there are flickers of memories of lifetimes before the most recent lifetime that are brought to mind but not completely recalled. At times there are individuals who have the choice before entering the physical life of having some kind of preview of the new life in the physical that they are about to enter. When they choose to reincarnate, they sometimes have a plan for the new life and sometimes do not.

People cannot come into their next lifetime more intelligent than in past lifetimes.

When people are born deaf or blind or in some way deformed, the reason for that condition is not necessarily something they have chosen at the soul level but it could be the result of karma or something that was chosen by themselves for their own advancement.

We have a choice to never reincarnate with certain people again but what we choose will not necessarily happen.

Before an entity reincarnates into the physical world, the entity first ascends from the spirit world to a realm where they lose their spirit body. They then receive a new spirit body before descending back into the spirit world and eventually back to the physical world.

When individuals reincarnate into a race different from that of the previous lifetime, they are not necessarily more likely to feel greater affinity to people of that race rather than to people of other races because it depends on the individual and the amount of prejudice in that individual.

People whom you consider to be your enemies in reality are often friends who, prior to reincarnation, agreed to help you with certain lessons that you needed to learn.

There is a connection between a person's physical ancestry and his reincarnations. Sometimes people reincarnate with members of their own families over and over again. It is not unusual for a person to be the reincarnation of an ancestor.

After a soul has had several difficult or unpleasant incarnations, they are able to have a pleasurable incarnation if they so choose.

Individuals sometimes choose to reincarnate for the purpose of working toward a noble goal for the betterment of others or mankind.

When a soul reincarnates, sometimes there are physical characteristics or features that carry over from one lifetime to another. If you had a very wide nose in one incarnation, for example, there is a possibility that you could have a wide nose in another incarnation.

When people cover themselves almost entirely with tattoos that give them a reptile like appearance, it is often a hidden memory of a previous incarnation on a different planet, another way of what they consider art work.

More Atlanteans are currently reincarnated in the yellow race than in other races.

The current Delhi lama is not the reincarnation of the previous Delhi lama.

The study of reincarnation evidence that Ian Stevenson made from the University of Virginia was very accurate.

Some people love or bond with animals more than they can with humans but that is not because they have recently transitioned from the animal kingdom to the human kingdom.

Jesus taught reincarnation even though very little is said about it in the Bible. Some books were not included in the Bible because they provided information about reincarnation. Such information would have lessened the control maintained by the Church.

Six hundred is a high number of lifetimes for a soul to have reincarnated on Earth. Most people have between 300 and 325 incarnations. 14 percent have fewer than 100 incarnations. Less than one percent has fewer than 10 incarnations. About 75 percent of the people have incarnations only on Earth rather than also on other planets. Advanced souls reincarnate more rapidly between lifetimes, often in less than 100 years between lifetimes; sometimes almost immediately.

# RELIGION AND CHRISTS

**Some of the information in this section has appeared in previous sections.**

There are more than 10,000 religions throughout the world today which developed as a result of the appearance of a specific entity, often an extraterrestrial. No religion was given to mankind directly from God.

After five thousand years from now, religion will no longer be necessary. It is necessary now; the main reason being to create comfort for the believers. It is also needed to help increase the level of morality among humans. Religion has been a necessary step for the elevation of humanity. It will be necessary after the Ascension for those who are taken off planet. It will not be needed by those who remain on Earth in the fourth density.

Christianity began after the appearance of Jesus, often referred to as Jesus the Christ, although Jesus himself had no idea that a new religion would come about because of what he taught. Christianity has taught us to believe that Jesus was the only Christ but that is far from true. There have been, are, and will be many Christs.

When two souls dwell in the same body, it is referred to as a split soul. The split soul can occur for the entire lifetime of the person or for a specific amount of time. One of the two souls in the same body can be a Christ spirit or a less evolved spirit.

Jesus was a split soul during the last three years of his ministry. He shared his body with the spirit of one of the 73 masters. A simplified definition of such a combination could be stated as the full manifestation of God in a way that could dwell in a human body

The Christ spirit does not enter the body suddenly all at once. It enters slowly but increasingly so that no shock occurs when it enters the body of the human. One soul is the human soul and the other is the Christ spirit.

Initially, and sometimes for the entire duration, the human is not aware that he is a Christ. There are 10,343 Christs in the world today. There have been untold numbers of instances when a human soul and the Christ spirit have dwelled in the same body.

Donald Trump is one such example. The Christ spirit is no longer with Donald Trump and his role has been completed. The Christ spirit withdrew from him because of his actions that were the result of his human personality. If Donald Trump had not allowed his own personality to dominate his actions, the Christ spirit would have stayed with him longer.

In his time Jesus was the most hated Christ of all, even more so than Trump. Abraham Lincoln was both a Christ and a president and the most hated president is our history; hated even more than Trump.

Mike Pence has a split soul with the Christ spirit but he is not aware that he is a split soul; the same as Trump's lack of awareness. He is destined to be a great president, as was Trump, and he will be such. The president after Pence will not be a split soul. History will treat both Trump and Pence as great presidents as it has treated Lincoln.

## Extraterrestrials in the Bible

Many events portrayed in the Old Testament of the Bible are actually a recounting of actual events or were allegories. There are some events that could be termed as made up stories. Some events did occur but were interpreted in a different way. For example, Jonah did not live three days inside a big fish. He was inside an extraterrestrial submarine.

Some of the people in the Bible were extraterrestrial beings that appeared as humans with the intent of the betterment of humankind. The same space people are involved here now as were in Biblical times. Many of the world's great religions today came about as the result of encounters with extraterrestrials, causing many of the confusions.

Jehovah was an extraterrestrial who gave the Ten Commandments directly to Moses. He guides and protects the Jews in modern times.

The following are some events portrayed in the Bible which involved the use of aliens or their technology:

Moses receiving the Ten Commandments
The burning bush on Mount Sinai
Ezekiel's account of a wheel within a wheel
The Ark of the Covenant
The walls of Jericho that crumbled
Jonah in the belly of a big fish

The Israelites crossing the Red Sea and the manna provided to the Jews in the wilderness were natural occurrences.

On some occasions, but not all, the accounts of angels in various cultures, including the Bible, were references to extraterrestrial beings.

The cause of the Great Flood that is mentioned in the Bible and in the lore of other ancient civilizations throughout the world was the accumulation of weather that had formed. It was not planned by aliens.

The origin of some of the rites and rituals of both the Catholicism and Judaism is connected with ancient extraterrestrial encounters with humans.

The information that was given to Joseph Smith, used for the basis of the Mormon religion, was not given to him by an angel but by an extraterrestrial.

## Religion and The Bible from the spirits point of view

Religion does not exist in the spirit world and after people cross over into that world, it is eventually no longer important to them. However, there are some spirits who do hold on to their religious beliefs from when they were humans. There is no religion in the spirit world because religion is manmade for different benefits of man. Spirits are too intelligent to take rules or guidance from religion.

People lose their religious beliefs when they enter the spirit world but the terrorists who have killed in the name of their religion still have the same attitudes but they don't have their religious beliefs.

There is no basis in reality for what some religions call purgatory.

After 1100 years from now religion will no longer play a significant role in the great majority of humans.

The meaning of the Trinity is that the Father is God, the Son is the human and the Holy Spirit is the Christ spirit.

There is no such thing as sin from the point of view of those in the spirit realm. Sin is purely a ridiculous religious concept.

Some of the ancient history portrayed in the Bible, including that of the Great Flood, is a recounting of earlier Sumerian legends.

There is much recounting of interesting stories in the Bible but some happened and some did not happen.

Some of what is in the Bible is taken from ideas presented in earlier civilizations and then embellished.

Even though much of the material in the New Testament of the Bible is not entirely factual, Christianity did nevertheless did serve the purpose of helping to raise the level of consciousness of the believers. In that aspect Christianity was a positive thing for those that got benefit.

Some of the prophets in the Bible were people who received information from extraterrestrials or the spirit world or even the Akashic records. The prophecies in the Bible and in the scriptures of other religions are essentially accurate although often misinter- preted.

Judas was portrayed as having betrayed Jesus in a way that would result in Jesus' crucifixion but he was greatly misunderstood. He was a friend of Jesus whose role was predestined.

The Biblical description of Adam and Eve and the Garden of Eden was just a story. It was a spaceship and the family lived there for many years.

The Nephilim were a race of giants of extraterrestrial origin that existed in Biblical times and Goliath was one of them but they were not the offspring of fallen angels. They were the offspring of tall humans from Jupiter who mated with earth men and women.

On some occasions, but not all, the accounts of angels in various cultures, including the Bible, were references to extraterrestrial beings.

The original purpose of male circumcision was simply to identify those men who were descendants of Adam or of the superhuman race that created them. The Jewish and Islam tradition of circumcism is a continuation of that tradition. They were not knowledgeable at that time about health reasons for performing circumcism. Abraham was not the first person to perform circumcism. Before him, circumcism was taking place for thousands of years.

The ten plagues of Egypt in the Bible were the result of a sequence of events of natural causes.

As a member of the royal family, there was a connection between Moses and King Akhenaton in ancient Egypt. He was the son of King Akhenaton and Queen Nefertiti. He was part extraterrestrial. It was because of the religious beliefs in one god and trying to change the religion of ancient Egypt that all traces of King Akhenaton and Queen Nefertiti were removed by the Egyptians after his death.

The Tower of Babel did not exist even though the Bible says that the proliferation of languages came about so that it became impossible for them to build the tower. The proliferation of languages occurred when humans went out of Africa to different parts of the world.

When the Israelites were crossing the desert they were able to eat many different plants growing there. A device called the Manna Machine described in the Jewish Kabala did not provide an algae type of food for the Jews when they wandered in the dessert because it did not exist.

It did not take the Israelites 40 years to cross the desert but it did take them 21 years. They intentionally prolonged their stay in the desert, one reason for which was to amass a large army for battling the various Canaanite groups in the reconquest of the land of Canaan.

The pillar of fire that guided the Jews through the desert was a UFO in the sky manipulated by extraterrestrials guiding them.

The Israelites were able to cross the Jordan River on the way to the Promised Land because the water was not deep and was full of pebbles on the bottom.

Moses was a cheerful man who was very humorous and had black skin, dark curly hair that was a little on the kinky side but he liked it long.

The Ark of the Covenant was in Egypt before Moses led the Israelites out of Egypt. There were several Arks of the Covenant which contained alien technology for defending the Jews. One of them still exists today but it is not in Israel. On the way to Canaan 77 people died when they came into contact with it. The ancient temple of Solomon housed the Ark of the Covenant.

The technology encased within the Ark of the Covenant was instrumental in bringing down the walls of Jericho. Amplified sound waves of the blowing of the trumpets caused the walls to melt. They did not just crumble but they liquefied and fell like mud. The Biblical account of this event is accurate for the most part.

The Stone of Scone that is placed under the throne of the British monarchy is not the pillow that Jacob slept on in the Bible.

Solomon's ring had what was viewed as supernatural powers. It was presented to him by extraterrestrials.

The people who call themselves the Lemba in Zimbabwe are actually descendants of one of what are called the lost tribes of Israel, the priestly tribe of the Cohens.

The Essenes did not originate on Atlantis but they originated 35 years before the birth of Jesus.

Lot's wife turned to ashes when she looked back at an atomic explosion.

The current world situation regarding the forces of good and evil are foretold in the scriptures of various religions. Prophets in the Bible provided information about the situation that is occurring at this moment.

There is a parallel between the current political situation involving the Clintons, President Obama and President Trump and King Ahab and Jezebel in our Bible. Hilary is the reincarnation of Jezebel and Bill is King Ahab.

Jesus taught reincarnation even though very little is said about it in the Bible. Certain books were not included in the Bible because they included information about reincarnation. The acceptance of reincarnation would lessen the control of the Church over humans.

In the Biblical story of Adam and Eve in the Garden of Eden, the serpent was of extraterrestrial origin and designed to be of a helpful nature.

The inspiration for speaking in Tongues comes from the mind. It is something that is built into the system of everyone who has a brain and it is a fantastic way of expressing oneself. In the charismatic church services where they speak in Tongues, they are actually allowing an extraterrestrial to speak through them which they themselves do not understand.

## Miscellaneous

Various religions existed among Earth people before the time of the Great Flood.

Many religions teach you that when you die you go immediately to either heaven or to hell but they say nothing about you going to the world of spirits.

People make their own heaven and they make their own hell. The spirit world is not heaven. Heaven and hell are purely religious concepts. They are not actual places but they are states of mind.

The acceleration of the demise of religion to some extent can be attributed to what we refer to as the New Age movement that was begun by Helena Blavatsky and the Theosophical movement which followed. She channeled information from both spirits and angels.

There is no such being that we call the devil. It exists only in the eyes of the beholder.

Lucifer was not an angel who had evil intentions. He was involved in the creation or the development of Earth humanity and was instrumental, in a way, in providing the tools for civilization. Lucifer's intent was to bring both good and evil. It depends on how you view things, whether it is good or bad. Lucifer brought knowledge to mankind that he shouldn't have given. Lucifer and Satan refer to the same entity.

It is not important to give special respect to cemeteries as hallowed ground. You do not have to treat cemeteries any different from any other area of Earth.

Throughout history a number of men have had stigmatas appear on the palms of their hands and on their foreheads which were believed to represent the wounds made in the crucifixion of Jesus but they actually represented disease.

Religions do not exist in any star systems in addition to Earth because religion is manmade.

Although many religions condemn gay marriages as being against the word of God, those marriages can be considered as natural as a marriage between a man and a woman. No condemnation should be made of homosexuality. Religions condemn gay marriages for the purpose of control and for not having children to increase the number of people in that religion.

The Cabal exerts more influence than the Alliance over churches. The churches are being controlled by forces that are not necessarily beneficial to humans. Churches are going in a more positive direction and they will become more meaningful. The big churches will become fewer in numbers.

The time will come when Christians, Jews and Moslems will exist peacefully without confrontations or warfare but in the not for several centuries.

Religion is very good for those who are not knowledgeable. There will be religious wars after many, many failures and many deaths.

The cause of anti-Semitism is often the result of extraterrestrials having spliced some of their own DNA into the DNA of humans.

# THE SOUL

In the beginning, God was just a consciousness without form. Creation occurred immediately when the consciousness became aware of itself. The consciousness then immediately exploded and became untold numbers of sparks of consciousness rather that a single consciousness. Each spark was the same as the original consciousness and was the beginning of a soul. Thus the soul began at the time of creation.

The God consciousness that that was the beginning of the soul is the basis of each soul. Initially the soul was just a consciousness. When this consciousness became aware of itself, the soul was capable of taking actions. The consequences of the actions are the beginning of the growth of the soul and the differentiation of individualities.

No two souls are alike. The soul is a complete entity unto itself. Soul mates and twin flames do not exist because the soul is strong enough to survive by itself and it doesn't need a mate.

The first action of the soul was to manifest itself in the mineral kingdom. After many reincarnations (i.e. re-mineralizations) in the mineral kingdom, the soul evolved into the vegetable kingdom where it also had many re-vegetabilizations.

The soul then manifested itself in the animal kingdom where reincarnation was a factor as it now is in the human kingdom. The human kingdom and the spirit realm are joined together. After manifesting as a human, the soul goes to the spirit realm where it continues to evolve before going back to the human kingdom.

After many incarnations in the human kingdom, the soul reaches a point where it no longer needs to reincarnate because it has achieved as much as it can from being in the physical body. From that point on, the soul is in a lighter body in the spirit world where it can stay for eons.

After there is no longer a need to reincarnate, some souls choose to come back to the physical world for the purpose of helping humanity, but not with the intent of elevating their own level of development. We refer to them as Christs.

After souls have reached the highest level in the spirit world, they move to realms above the spirit realm. The first realm above the spirit realm is the mental realm, a very personal world where the soul does not have relationships with other souls. There are four realms above the mental realm. In all, there are seven levels of evolution including the human level.

## The evolution of the soul

The soul is the only permanent thing that distinguishes one individual from another. Souls are dynamic and forever changing by the information that is fed to them through the physical or spirit form. All human souls part of a greater soul.

The soul created the physical body so the physical body could have input into the development of the soul. The same is true of the spirit form. The physical body is used to provide information for the soul and then the physical body passes away. The same is true of the spirit body. The physical form is just temporary and the spirit form is just temporary. The physical body is not our real self and the spirit body is not our real self.

There is a big difference between the spirit and the soul. The spirit form intervenes between the physical body and the soul. The soul is more controlling than the spirit. The evolution of a soul does not reach a limit but it just goes on evolving endlessly. After an inconceivable number of years humans can eventually evolve to the God level.

New souls are still continuing to come into existence in the mineral kingdom.

Fragments of the soul are right from the beginning of time. This means that elements or fragments of a soul are in the mineral kingdom and the vegetable kingdom and then those elements coalesce upon the entry into the animal kingdom.

Souls are never totally dissolved; but when judged irredeemable they must return to their perfect fragmented state and then have to start over again in the mineral or the vegetable kingdom.

Old souls are souls that have had many lifetimes. Since old souls are people who have had many previous incarnations, we tend to think of them as being wiser and more evolved than the others but that is not correct. They are old souls simply because they have been slow learners and must repeatedly reincarnate.

They are slow learners because they ignore things that they think are unimportant. Sometimes the unimportant may be the vessel to the most important. If we pay attention to things that may not seem important we might not be such a slow learner and we might not have to have further lifetimes. Just because we are an old soul does not mean that we are more highly evolved than newer souls. Some souls evolve more rapidly on the spirit plateau.

Some souls have multiple simultaneous incarnations because they want to progress more rapidly. They advance more rapidly when they have several simultaneous incarnations. It depends upon the individual soul whether it can have multiple simultaneous incarnations. Souls are more likely to have multiple simultaneous incarnations when a major shift of Earth energy is about to occur. There are more multiple simultaneous incarnations than in the past because of the impending Ascension that will be completed in the year 11,962.

When people commit suicide they are disappointed with the life that they have created. In most cases, the soul will not rest when death was not a naturally planned incident. Those who commit suicide are uncomfortable and suicide is not always a comfortable although an easy way out. Suicide can also be a severe detriment to an individual's evolution because others around them could be negatively affected.

A soul can, through agreement with another soul, willingly leave the body permanently and return to the spirit realm so that another soul can take over that body until it dies in order to perform a specific predetermined role. It's what we call walk-ins, a change of personality. The walk-in retains the memory of the walk-out because memories are stored in the cells of the body. The walk-out is a change of who they were and no longer wish to be.

Walk-ins are not always souls who incarnate for the purpose of benefitting mankind. They sometimes incarnate simply to complete an unfinished task from a previous incarnation. Souls that walk out often leave because they have completed the task for which they incarnated. Sometimes they just don't like the life they are living and just want to get out of it. Walk-ins and walk-outs are not always planned between lifetimes.

A split soul is half a walk-in and half not. An individual can be two personalities at the same time, the original and the new personality.

All souls will eventually evolve as far as a human can evolve; to the state of completion or perfection as a human. At that point they become the Christ Spirit.

The noblest of souls' purposes in both the spirit world and ours is to be of service to others.

All souls are part of a greater soul, similar to the way that a soul can have multiple simultaneous incarnations. Therefore we could say that all souls are connected and that each soul's actions have an effect on other souls. Those in the spirit world are part of this.

The soul does not suffer when a fetus is intentionally aborted because it knows in advance that the fetus will be aborted. Abortion is not a negative act.

DNA can be used to trace our ancestry lineage and also for soul lineage or ancestry. The soul changes when the DNA of humans is modified. Bursts of energy from the sun can change a person's DNA. DNA is part of the soul as well as part of the physical body.

We can learn to expand our consciousness to a higher level if we learn to relax. To meditate is to listen to the God in our soul.

Our thinking, feelings, and our entire personality all dwell in our soul and within the structure of the earth. They contribute to the level of consciousness of the earth.

Those who listen to much of the current popular music such as hip-hop or rap can lower their level of Intelligence. This is an activity of the Cabal. People can increase their level of what we call spirituality or evolution by listening to classical music if that calms them.

Some reincarnations can occur immediately. The average time between incarnations is about 300 years and the maximum time is 9,850 years unless a soul chooses to reincarnate to help humanity after the soul has reached the point where incarnation is no longer necessary.

The length of time between re-mineralizations in the mineral kingdom and re-vegetabilizations in the vegetable kingdom is about the same as it is for reincarnations in the animal kingdom.

After we evolve to the seventh level, which some call the seventh heaven, the evolution of the soul continues. A similar process begins again but at a higher level. That process is repeated seven times. This process continues forever with no end to the evolution of the soul until it becomes at one with the creator.

As we evolve we become God, as great a God as the creator. We become creators of a whole new universe. The same process begins all over again with each creation. The process is unending.

Soul groups, also referred to as soul families, are usually composed of about 25 to 75 entities but not all of those entities incarnate together. There is usually some kind of karma to be experienced between various members who incarnate together.

Karma can be both positive and/or negative. There can be both positive and negative karma involved in the same relationship. Positive karma creates situations designed to be pleasant or helpful. Negative karma presents opportunities which must be resolved by the exercise of the free will of those involved. The same is true of positive karma. Karma itself is like electricity, neither positive nor negative.

Before you reincarnate you can plan to meet someone that you had known

# SPIRITS

## Personality traits of the spirits

People in the spirit world have the same kinds of emotions as those in our world. Some are happy, sad, or grouchy. Jealousy exists in the spirit realm, just as in the physical world when one human is envious of another.

There are lazy spirits and there are ambitious spirits and spirits that are not aware. Just as some humans have very strong will power and others have weak will power, the same is true of spirits. Like humans, some spirits are immature and playful and other spirits are very serious with little sense of humor.

There is not a whole lot of difference between the range of humans and the range of spirits regarding the level of intelligence. Spirits sometimes have memory problems and forget things they would normally be expected to remember, just as do people.

Humans that have mental or emotional disorders carry over those same disorders when they arrive on in the spirit world. There are times they can overcome them when they cross over. Anything is possible. It depends upon the individual. Just as in the physical world, there are emotionally disturbed spirits also. When the person becomes a spirit he doesn't go into a state of perfection.

There are humans whose thinking process is distorted and also spirits who do not think logically. One's crossing over does not mean there's going to be a change. There can be awareness but that does not mean there's going to be a change. If one is ignorant one will remain that way. Spirits can evolve after they cross over if they wish. Just because they have passed on does not mean they are correct.

Just as many humans can be quite egotistical and not much concerned for other people, the same is true after they enter the spirit world.

There are no rules or no such thing as right or wrong in the spirit world but spirits can still be judgmental.

**Spirits' capabilities**

Spirits can perceive the physical world as it is now only through the senses of sound and smell. They cannot see the physical world as it is now.

Spirits are able to view scenes from their life when they were in the physical, such as their home as it was when they were a child. They could go back in time and actually visit or in some way feel their home as it was then.

Spirits are able to go back and witness or re-experience past events such as President Kennedy's assassination. Since time does not exist in the spirit world, spirits generally have a greater degree of patience than those in our world.

It makes no difference if it is in the near future or the far future for spirits to accurately predict events but since the element of time does not exist in the spirit dimension, they are not able to predict the timing of future events.

Spirits are often able to recall events of their most recent physical life more vividly and with greater clarity than they can with their memories while they are in the physical. They can recall events from many of their lifetimes in the physical if they so choose. Most of them are not interested in recalling events of past lives or virtually relive past events. They see what they want to see.

Spirits can create their own personal world; whatever they want just by thinking it and then wanting it; whereas in the physical world a third step is needed; taking some kind of action. What they create appears just as solid to them as objects in the physical world are to us.

Spirits have differing amounts of energy; the more highly evolved souls, the greater the level of energy. The amount of energy they possess determines the extent to which they can help humans. Spirits refer to themselves as energy beings and can perceive the level of energy of other spirits.

Jesus has a very high energy level and there are entities with a level of energy similar to that of Jesus, and even more. Jesus is called most often and he has the energy for that. There are times spirits need to rest in order to restore our energy. They use their energy to help others

Spirits can instantaneously be in the presence of or be in contact with any other entities they choose. They can be in more than one place at the same time and can also be in different time periods simultaneously, whether past or future. They are able to communicate simultaneously with more than one person or spirit.

It is easier for spirits to show themselves to some people than it is for them to show themselves to other people. That is, spirits have to use more energy for some people to see them and less energy for others to see them. They can create what we view as miracles.

Spirits cannot exorcise evil spirits from places or people in our realm. Only humans can do that. It is more important for humans to exorcise them.

If a person has never had a physical incarnation in a certain star system, that person is still able to go to the spirit realm of that star system after he disincarnates.

If your grandfather were to reincarnate into the physical world as another personality, your other relatives in the spirit world would not still have contact with him as the personality of your grandfather.

Spirits are at times better able to see and understand themselves more accurately than when they were in the physical world. All spirits can do such, not just those in the higher level.

Sometimes when people pass over to the spirit world they are able to communicate with humans immediately and sometimes they have to wait a while until they are ready to do so.

Spirits have the ability to hear and read the minds of humans as soon as the spirit crosses over. They can read each other's minds without using their senses.

Spirits often communicate with people at night time because their conscious minds are less active. Many people sleep restlessly because lost souls are trying to contact them for help

Some spirit guides are more competent than others because they are more evolved.

Spirits have the same five senses but they use them in a different way.

Spirits can disappear or evaporate, just like you think you are seeing something for a moment and then look again and it is not visible to your eyes. A medium can actually see the spirits in their true forms.

**Spirits' connection with other spirits**

When a person crosses over to the spirit world and encounters former friends and relatives, they do not have the same type of relationship with them as they had when they were in the physical, such as a parent/child relationship. There is a new kind of connection. They don't consider their human parents to be their parents in any way.

Some friendships in the spirit world are carryovers from previous incarnations and some are not. Just as with humans, spirits like some spirits and dislike others.

Spirits can perceive the personality of spirits they encounter. They can sense the emotions of other spirits. They can perceive past life personalities of those they encounter but only past lives, not future lives.

Spirits usually perceive other spirits in the personality of their most recent lifetime because that lifetime comes in very forceful but their recent lifetime is not necessarily their strongest. Spirits have the ability to choose which personality they wish to show to other spirits or mediums.

Spirits do not always tell the truth but they know when others are lying to them or trying to deceive them. A spirit cannot hide from another spirit.

There are times that when a spirit creates something with the mind, such as a reproduction of a physical home when that creation is perceivable by other spirits.

Spirits can sometimes combine their energies so that they can have enough energy to create an apparition dense enough for humans who are not mediums to see.

Spirits need not verbalize because they can sense the minds of others but they can speak verbally to each other using the language called Tongues.

There are some spirits whom they like and some whom they dislike; some they trust and some they distrust. They pick their own friends.

Spirits have names in the spirit world by which other spirits can make contact with them or refer to them.

Spirits who have similar interests band together to work toward a common goal.

As in the physical world, there are leaders in the spirit world if they wish. Spirits select those that they put on a pedestal if they wish to put someone on a pedestal. It is not completely true that there is no one in charge because the only person that is in charge is one's self.

Spirits feel more connected with each other than humans feel toward each other and they blend much more.

In the spirit world, people of the same type tend to stay together because they agree on the issues. They tend to associate with those similar to themselves as far as their level of evolution.

## Spirits' connection with humans and other entities

Angels play a role in the existence of spirits by guiding them and administering to them just as they do for humans. In order to protect humans, spirits can project thoughts into the minds of those who want to cause humans harm.

Spirits are able to communicate with entities in realms above or beyond the plateau on which they are. Those on higher realms than spirits can see more and do more than spirits. Sometimes more can be seen from the lower realms.

Spirits can communicate with animals in the physical world as well as with animals in the spirit realm. They can Influence animals too.

Highly evolved spirits can manifest themselves as physical human beings that anyone can see. They are not angels but they can manifest themselves for a brief moment with their energy. All spirits wish for more energy.

Spirits are aware of the karma of humans even though humans may not be aware of their own karma.

When a person is about to cross over to the spirit world, spirits know this in advance and are aware and ready to welcome and assist them.

Relationships don't always continue when souls transfer from the spirit world to the physical world. Sometimes relationships can start in the spirit world and can continue in the physical word but don't always appear to be so.

Spirits can learn from those in the physical world. They can learn by "reading" this book.

In the spirit world there are times that an individual can like people and other times dislike them. They can like humans but not like what they are thinking of doing. Spirits have reactions similar to those of humans. Some people are negative, and spirits do pick up our thoughts.

It is not always a definite future when spirits see the future of humans because humans have free will. Therefore future actions cannot always be predicted with 100 percent accuracy. Usually actions will occur but the time they occur cannot be predicted because time does not exist in the spirit world.

When people cross over to the spirit world and then discover that a trusted friend had been dishonest with them when they were together in the physical, spirits sometimes become vengeful toward those in the physical world. They are like humans. They neither forgive nor forget.

Some spirits seek to have humans worship them but they are not bad spirits. Some spirits feel temptations, such as wanting to be put on a pedestal by humans but they do not give into those temptations.

When a spirit manifests itself to humans, it can appear in whatever form it chooses, similar to how the angels manifest themselves. A spirit could manifest itself as both a living object and an inanimate object. Like an angel, a spirit could manifest itself as lightning, a car, an animal or anything else.

Spirits do not read the actual thoughts that are in the conscious minds of humans because their word thinking can change. They do read the intent behind the thoughts that are accessed from the subconscious mind.

Demons do not exist in the spirit world. They are only for humans. There are no parasites in the spirit realm that feed off of the negative energy created by humans. They don't allow it. They just reject it from the very beginning.

Just as spirits assist humans, humans can be of assistance to spirits. They can do that by helping each other, not necessarily by helping the spirit directly. Therefore when humans help humans, they are actually helping spirits.

The work of the spirits is to help humans by making us happy, making us feel comfortable.

Humans can drain a spirit's energy but they can also add to a spirit's energy by showing love and kindness and showing how well they are progressing. It is human interactions with other humans that elevate the level of energy of spirits.

The actions of all human can be perceived by the spirits. That doesn't necessarily mean that spirits want to observe humans all the time.

If humans don't want spirits to know what they are doing, say "Please go away and leave in peace." and the spirit will leave

Humans are concerned about the conflict between the Cabal and the Alliance and the spirits are also concerned. The conflict is affecting the spirit world as well as the physical world.

Spirits perceive and communicate with nature spirits such as fairies, gnomes, elves and leprechauns. It just happens naturally.

## Spirits' attitudes, emotions and desires

In regard to whether life in the spirit world is easier or more pleasurable than it is in the physical world, it depends on the route that spirits take. If they choose to take a difficult route, then life would be difficult but would provide them with the opportunity to evolve more rapidly.

Life in the spirit world can be more pleasant than life in the physical world because it's very simple and easier. Many of the religions developed the concept of heaven because life is so much easier in the spirit world.

There are many levels in the spirit world and when people cross over to that world, they reside at the level which matches their actions when they were in the physical world.

As with humans, more advanced spirits are less influenced by their emotions than are the less advanced souls. Spirits have emotions and feelings too and they love to give advice.

Like humans, spirits sometimes do or say things that they later regret.

Although spirits do not experience physical pain, they can experience emotional pain.

If individuals were obsessed with sex while in the physical, after they cross over they take pleasure in observing the sexual activities of humans.

There are many differences among spirits just as there are among humans

When a spirit serves as a guide to a human, it is considered a noble endeavor. Guides sometimes feel relieved when the person crosses over and they don't have to guide anymore. Some spirits don't always like the person but they succeed in being there for him. Spirits have no input regarding for whom they will serve as a guide.

Some spirits are gregarious and enjoy being with others but there are also some who are not very sociable and prefer being alone or having very little contact with others. Like humans, there are also spirits that tend to be loners. In both worlds loners are fearful individuals.

Spirits have combinations of thinkers, some more liberal and some more conservative in their thinking.

There is a wide range of intelligence among spirits just as there is among humans. Some are more intelligent and some are just stupid.

There are spirits who are nosy and like to pry into everyone else's business but spirits don't read minds for entertainment. They mean to be helpful.

Like humans, spirits have different opinions about situations or how to answer a question, or what to do. There are varying opinions among spirits regarding the social issues of Earth people, such as gay marriages.

The use of numerology by spirits is not an effective device for providing answers, explanations or predictions as it is for us. Numbers are important because they can be fun and helpful to work with. There is significant negativity in the number 666. It is not just something that religion has invented. Conversely, the number 7 is a very positive number.

If people like to travel and explore various cultures and places throughout the world, it is likely that they will still derive pleasure from doing that when they are in the spirit world. Most spirits enjoy visiting places in the physical world.

People who are inquisitive will remain inquisitive in the spirit world.

When a person is in the spirit world, he has no emotional attachments to the dates of his birth or his death from when he was in the physical.

The place where a person died has no significance or purpose after they have crossed over. It is just another place to be put at rest without any meaning to them. The meaning of where they have lived is more important but the place where they died is not.

In both worlds true love could be defined as when we care about someone else more than we care about ourselves.

After a spouse dies and enters the spirit world, spirits do not become upset when the human spouse enters into a relationship with a new person because spirits are complete entities and do not need a mate. Since spirits are no longer confined to their physical being, they do not want to hold on to their physical spouse. In fact there are times that the spirit is relieved to have gotten rid of their spouse.

When a baby is born, it usually is a joyful experience to humans and the same true in the spirit world when a person transitions to their world. Spirits are indeed at times joyous to receive if those who enter are pleasant people but that is just a momentary fact.

It is possible for an individual to overcome physical addictions while in the spirit world if they realize that there is an issue. Like humans, most spirits do not realize that they have issues. Issues do not necessarily have to reoccur in a subsequent lifetime as karma.

In the spirit world helping humans and helping those when they cross over is their work and is entertainment for them.

Spirits sometimes need rest to restore their energy but they do not sleep in a physical sense. They withdraw unto themselves and do not communicate with others.

When there is a major disaster such as an earthquake or a tsunami in our world in which many people are killed, they are aware of what is to be and are always there to welcome those who are coming into their world.

There are no places in the universe where spirits cannot or are forbidden to go. They have full freedom to go anywhere in the universe and can do that instantaneously.

When there are spirits in a house, electrical appliances can be activated by them. Although they cannot control this, they do have fun doing so. Appliances can sometimes be activated even when they are not connected to an electrical outlet.

Spirits can manipulate objects in the physical world much the same as earthbound poltergeists do. The pendulum is the easiest object for a spirit to move.

## Miscellaneous

High energy evil entities exist in the spirit realm. Evil is not knowledgeable. It is ignorance.

Since stars, planets and other celestial bodies exist in the physical world, they also exist in the spirit world. Astrology has influence in the spirit world as it does in our world. Astrology always existed and always was helpful but spirits do not make use of it although it is actually effective in the physical world. The date of a person's entry into the astral world has an influence on his personality while as a spirit.

A person who has experienced severe emotional problems all his life and is unaware of the cause of the disturbance can learn the cause of those problems after entering the spirit world if they are not emotionally disturbed.

In order for a spirit to serve as a guide, a spirit must not necessarily have completed the required reincarnation cycle. Serving as a guide to humans helps the personal growth or advancement of the guide. Service to others helps both spirits and humans to achieve their purpose in life; that is to evolve more rapidly.

When a person who has had an incarnation on several different planets dies, that spirit resides in the astral realm of the planet of his most recent lifetime.

# SPIRITS THAT ARE EARTHBOUND

Earthbound spirits are people who have died but, for various reasons, do not go directly into the spirit word. They are in a place that we call the in-between world. In some cases it is just for a short period of time and in other cases it can be for a longtime, even what seems like forever. Earthbound spirits can be either of a positive nature or of a negative nature.

We use the term ghost to refer to spirits that are earthbound for a long period of time and are temporarily trapped there. Some of them can be simultaneously part in the in-between world and part in the spirit world.

When a person dies he has a choice whether or not to remain earthbound. That decision is not made by forces beyond the person's control but by the person himself.

It is important for people to enlighten earthbound spirits and encourage them to move on by speaking aloud even when they do not see them.

When a spirit becomes earthbound, souls from the other side who love them come forth and help that spirit cross over to the spirit world. There is always help from the other side to help them when they cross over.

Upon death about 62 percent of people move directly into the spirit world and about 38 percent of them linger in the in-between world before moving to the spirit world. 28 percent linger for less than a year. 3 percent linger for more than ten years. Some remain between the two worlds for more than 100 years.

It can be advantageous or desirable for a person to knowingly remain earthbound for a while before crossing over to the spirit world. It is not of advantage for a spirit to stay earthbound for a while when not needed because there a danger that the spirit will become trapped in the earthbound realm. It is best to go as soon possible into the spirit world.

Entities can remain earthbound for several reasons. At times it is possible that the person might want to oversee, for example, the work on a project he had been working on until it is completed by others. It depends upon the individual.

Sometimes they need our permission to go to the spirit world. We can do this by talking aloud to them as if they were still in the physical and telling them we will be okay without them. Earth people who excessively mourn them often hold back the person from proceeding forward.

Another reason for not going directly into the spirit world is that they are unaware that they have died and are lost and don't know what to do. We should speak aloud to them as if they were still in the physical, telling them that they have died and we will miss them but they should move on to the spirit world by following the light.

Most of the time when individuals are not aware that they are deceased, they will move on once they realize they have died. They are usually in a very much confused state of mind.

Some spirits remain earthbound because they fear that they will go to hell if they follow the light, perhaps because of their religion. Any kind of fear could also be a reason why they remain earthbound.

There are things that earthbound spirits can experience that a soul which has entered the spirit world cannot experience.

They sometimes wish to stay on the earth to cause problems.

Earthbound spirits do not hold themselves to the place that they are buried. They do not suffer in the cemetery but that is simply the place where we have placed them, not where they want to be.

There are occasions when part of a person's consciousness remains with the body at the gravesite for a while. We do not have to fear cemeteries because ghosts are not there. They are, however, sometimes attracted to the place where they have died.

If someone died many years ago and at that time their house was a small cabin and now it has been rebuilt as a large house, the earthbound spirit will see the house as it was a cabin, not as it now is.

The spirits of children who experienced a tragic death are often likely to remain earthbound longer than other earthbound spirits and they are likely to show themselves to other children.

Sometimes earthbound spirits who have not fully crossed over into the spirit realm can foresee the future the same as those in the spirit world do and sometimes they can't.

People who live to a very old age and have no close friends or relatives are not necessarily less likely to remain earthbound than people who die in the prime of their lives. Even though they have no friends on Earth, they can remain earthbound before going on to the spirit world if they wish to be that way.

Earthbound spirits can influence a person's thinking to help them just as those in the spirit world can do.

If a person can see earthbound spirits, they can also see other spirits.

Earthbound spirits sometimes materialize to ask for help from those in the physical world. They also can want to control, which can be either good or bad for the person in the physical world.

The use of tarot cards can provide an entry for an earthbound spirit to communicate or in some way make its presence known to humans. There could be danger in using tarot cards in regard to calling in negative spirits, depending on what they are used for. Ouija boards are definitely more harmful than tarot cards.

Children's imaginary friends are not imaginary but are usually earthbound spirits and they are real friends. They are usually playful, not destructive.

When earthbound spirits repeatedly do the same thing, such as moving the same object again and again, that action is usually to let people know of their presence.

Earthbound spirits must follow physical laws of the physical world, such as turning a doorknob and pushing the door in order to enter a room but they need energy, a great deal of energy to do that. They like to move chairs and other objects also.

Some earthbound spirits can inflict physical injury, such as scratches, on a person.

Animals, especially dogs, have an innate ability to perceive the presence of earthbound spirits.

The room temperature often drops when an earthbound spirit is present because it is easier for them to communicate in coolness.

The pilot and the engineer of Eastern Airlines flight 401 that crashed in the Florida Everglades in 1972 appeared as earthbound entities on other airplanes which used parts that were salvaged from that crashed plane. The parts that were used in other airplanes attracted them to the airplane and the men were seen on a number of airplanes that used those parts. They were seen as shadows.

There is usually a disturbance in electromagnetic energy in the vicinity of earthbound spirits. This can and will be measured with available technology.

There are physical entryways to the in-between world for humans who are sensitive to such.

Sometimes earthbound spirits attach themselves to a person and are able to experience the world through the senses of that person with all the physical senses.

People who have committed suicide are usually not at rest and are hurting not only themselves but their soul.

The more education we have about earthbound spirits, the more prepared we will be if we are ever confronted with one.

If a ghost passes through a person's body, that person can feel the energy pass through him even if the ghost is not seen. It is often a cold energy.

Demons are very negative entities that attach themselves to people to scare them or hurt them. They are usually a part of someone that performed nefarious deeds when they were in the physical world. After attaching themselves to a person, they can remain dormant until many years later when something arouses them.

Demons can be removed through exorcism. If a person becomes religious, that is not the cause of awakening the demon. Fear within the person is usually the action that will activate the demon. Demons can only harm you if you believe in them.

Demons can show themselves to humans as either male or female even though spirits don't have gender. Demons can attach themselves to a person at any time, even while they are still in the womb. They can attach themselves to specific organs. A person can be simultaneously possessed by multiple demons. We can also attract demons to ourselves by our thoughts.

Demons can attach themselves to objects and places as well as to people. They can harm us but they cannot force anyone to do anything we don't want to do at the subconscious level. They try to deceive us by showing themselves in whatever form they choose. They don't show their faces because they want to scare us more.

At times it is possible for people to sense the presence of demons in other people. Demons have names but they do not want their names to be known. They do not exist in the spirit world but they are only for humans. People who have strong will power can avoid having demons attach themselves. We can absolutely be stronger than demons and we should not fear them. Even though demons appear strong, they are really weak.

The majority of ghosts are harmless to humans. There are rules that ghosts must play by and a limit to how far they can go. No earthbound spirit can have control over you if you do not allow it.

The wanting or not wanting comes from the subconscious level rather than the conscious level.

Poltergeists are ghosts that have enough energy to make noises and make objects move. They can do anything they wish to scare the hell out of you if that is what they are trying to do. Some poltergeists can be negative and others not negative. They can be negative when they wish to have control. Poltergeists are mostly negative entities or just children or pranksters. They sometimes make things move just to get your attention.

Poltergeists get their energy to move physical objects and cause various kinds of havoc and damage in our world by drawing on their own anger or other strong emotions. They can become energized to the extent that they can be heard or move physical objects. Their energy is very strong in what they want to say to you. They want to say it over and over and repeat it over and over. They want you to hear them.

Fear or other negative emotions of people make it easier for poltergeists to perform their activities. If they do not get control of you, negative poltergeists usually become angry. They can make things, such as blood, appear in the physical world.

Poltergeists are frequently the victim of a violent death, such as a murder or tragic accident. A poltergeist's actions do not result in the death of a person but rather indirectly because of the actions of a fear-filed person.

Poltergeists sometimes show themselves when they are making objects move and some people can actually see the spirit. Their voices can be heard by people, not just by those who are mediums.

It is possible but rare for poltergeists to follow people when they move from one home to another rather than remaining in the original home. They more often remain in the same place but they can move.

Teenagers often provide an easier entryway for poltergeists than do other people because they are more easily influenced. Some adults can be easily influenced also. Babies can become poltergeists when they die.

Malevolent spirits can attach themselves to a person and influence them to perform evil deeds. The use of Ouija boards can definitely unleash evil spirits that can take possession of a person or bring about negative happenings.

Animals can be possessed by evil spirits and they can be earthbound and not cross over.

The danger in taking drugs or alcohol is more than just a physical danger. It is dangerous for a person to imbibe large quantities of alcohol or take mind altering drugs. Doing so makes it easier for negative spirits to influence or attach themselves to people when they are in a weakened condition.

It is easier for an evil entity to take possession of a person who has been hypnotized.

An evil spirit can take over a person and make the person's facial features appear slightly different or endow him with supernatural strength.

A person can speak certain specific words or phrases that have the power to remove negative spirits. "No" is one such word. A powerful phrase is to get a spirit to go away is "Leave in peace."

Depending on the energy of a person, ancient Egyptian mummies or artifacts from their tombs can bring negative energies to people. If conditions are right they can affect people. However, it is nonsense to believe that a mummy can take possession of a person. The degree of influence depends on the weakness of the person.

There are books that give effective instructions for conjuring up evil spirits. If people follow the instructions in a book, they can actually conjure up an evil spirit. Dangerous situations can be created, especially by the use of the pentagram.

Dark forces that affect humans can emanate from anywhere in the universe, not just from Earth. A single diabolical entity can simultaneously manifest itself as multiple diabolical entities.

Objects, such as a car, can be possessed or haunted by earthbound spirits and there also places that are haunted. When a place is haunted by earthbound spirits, people often become depressed, withdrawn or frightened to the extent that their personality can be affected.

If an earthbound spirit haunts a house and then that house is torn down and replaced by a new house, that entity can haunt the new house. It is often the land, rather than the building, to which the entity is attracted. The land is essential but the building doesn't really matter. The entity will haunt the earth until it finds peace.

It is possible but not probable that the presence of a specific person living in a home is the only reason that an earthbound entity haunts a house.

Even though some people feel that it is nonsense, religious articles or religious scriptures read aloud are useful in exorcisms of poltergeists and demons. One means of exorcizing an evil spirit is to pick up a cross and hold it close to you. That will work even though you don't believe in the cross or are doubtful of its potential.

Evoking the name of Jesus Christ can help exorcise an evil spirit who possesses a person. It is absolutely effective in cleansing a place, and powerful. If you were to use that name, or any other name that has power, it would have the same effect as a priest using it.

Sage is functional for the cleansing of a house from earthbound spirits. Water itself is also good for cleansing. It does not have to be what some people think of as holy water.

Spirits cannot exorcise evil spirits from places or humans. Only humans can exorcise them.

Demons can usually be exorcised trough the rituals of the Catholic Church even though the person is not of that religion.

When a person has a near death experience, there is an increased likelihood that the person will pick up a spirit attachment. Sometimes that attachment will remain with the person after the near death experience and sometimes not.

Ordinary cameras can sometimes photograph earthbound spirits that the human eyes cannot see. Ordinary sound recorders pick up sounds from them that humans cannot hear. Thermal imaging cameras are definitely a means of detecting earthbound spirits.

# TECHNOLOGY

## Ancient technology

Some of the information in this section appeared in *ANCIENT HISTORY*

In ancient times was there a global wireless energy network throughout the world that was used by extraterrestrials and by previous civilizations of Earth peoples. All star systems need similar kinds of energies. The energy system that was on Earth was used in other parts of the universe.

There have been previous human civilizations on Earth before Atlantis that were more intelligent and technologically advanced than our current civilization.

The Atlanteans had advanced technologies and they were interested in building and the mechanics of their building. They were very imaginative but we are doing quite well since the time of the typewriter.

They had air travel but they did not need ground vehicles for transportation. Flying machines powered by crystals were much easier.

Humans of long ago used the power of sound, taught to them by extraterrestrials, to accomplish such feats as moving extremely heavy objects. Sound was used in the construction of some of the unusual ancient monuments we find throughout the world. It was used in the construction of the great pyramids. It was the frequency of the sound and the volume. Sound was also used to move stones at Stonehenge. Edward Leedskalnin used sound to raise those heavy stones to build the Coral Castle in Homestead Florida.

We have noted that certain opera singers can break drinking glasses simply by using their voice.

The Ark of the Covenant in the Bible produced energy. There is an Ark of the Covenant which still exists today deep in the earth today securely inaccessible on Oak Island in Nova Scotia. There were several Arks of the Covenant that were used as weapons. In Biblical times, the Philistines stole an Ark of the Covenant and then suffered the serious consequences of its effects. After the return of the Ark of the Covenant from the Philistines, 77 people died when they looked at it.

The technology encased within the Ark of the Covenant when the Israelites went around the walls of Jericho was instrumental in bringing them down. It contained alien energy producing technology. It was amplified sound waves of the blowing of the trumpets to cause the walls to simply melt like mud. The Biblical account of this event is accurate except that the walls did not crumble but rather melted like mud. No Arks of the Covenant are now in Israel.

People were knowledgeable about the creation of and the use of electricity in Biblical times and they were able to harness it. The ancient pyramids were used to create electricity. There was electric lighting in the ancient tombs in Egypt and they made use of other electrical devices also.

Antigravity technology exists today and it was used in the construction of ancient structures.

In ancient times there were occasions in which great numbers of people were killed by radiation from atomic explosions caused by people on Earth, such as in Mohenjo-Daro Pakistan.

The ancient Egyptians were able to perform brain surgery. They had some assistance from aliens but they were able to progress on their own.

The ancient Egyptians tried to create gold by the transformation of other minerals in the pyramid at Giza but they were not successful.

The ancient civilization in India possessed information about aviation that was more advanced than that of today. Sanskrit writings could teach us how to advance our knowledge of aviation.

Highly sophisticated robots existed on Earth in the ancient past.

Some of the ancient structures on Earth were built by melting rock and then reformed by putting it into molds.

What the ancients viewed as magic was actually advanced technology.

Laser technology existed in the ancient world.

**Involvement of the spirits and extraterrestrials**

Some of the information in this section appeared in *EXTRATERRESTRIALS*

Throughout history the majority of great scientists have been influenced by extraterrestrials.

Many of the creations made by humans did not emanate from their own minds but they were influenced by external sources.

Thomas Edison received a great deal of information from extraterrestrial sources. Information about electricity was given to him.

Extraterrestrials are having a great deal more influence than we might realize on the thinking of humans because they can project their thoughts into our minds.

Einstein used his psychic ability to develop the Theory of Relativity. His work was attributable to both his high IQ and assistance from extraterrestrials in developing that theory.

Steve Jobs, the founder of Apple Computer, received information about his inventions from extraterrestrials and he took it with him when he left the physical world.

Nicolai Testa was a brilliant man who received advice regarding electricity from both spirits and extraterrestrials.

During World War II both the Axis and the Allied powers used psychics and channelers to assist them in their war efforts. There was assistance or influence from extraterrestrials.

The Nazis received technology information indirectly from the extraterrestrials through reverse engineering of their crashed UFO's. They lost the war because they were deliberately misled by opposing extraterrestrials.

Many of our technologies have been achieved through analyzing equipment found on crashed UFO's.

The United States government is involved in programs of reverse engineering of alien spacecraft or other alien technology. They are examining things they found and then cover them. The development of the transistor in the 1940's came from reverse engineering of objects found in crashed UFOs.

There is currently technology that was retrieved from UFOs in the hands of nations which we consider our enemies, such as Iran, Russia, China, and North Korea. Some of that technology is dangerous and could lead to warfare.

Spirits can be knowledgeable about technologies they never knew during their lifetimes in the physical. All modern communication technologies such as computers and Wi-Fi were inspired to humans by extraterrestrials and by spirits who previously experienced embodiment on more advanced worlds.

Plato had all of these advanced capabilities like electricity.

The earth has been visited by machines that humans believed were biological entities. There have been robots on Earth that were thought to be humans that were from extraterrestrials. Highly advanced extraterrestrial civilizations have absolutely been able to imbue robots with some degree of consciousness.

Liquid mercury was used in the propulsion systems of UFO's to counteract the effects of gravity. The liquid mercury that was found in the pyramids of Teotihuacan in Mexico was used for UFO propulsion.

Extraterrestrials have placed artificial satellites that orbit around the earth for our protection and also for giving them information about what is happening on Earth. The Van Allen radiation belt that surrounds the earth was placed there by extraterrestrials.

The Nazis actually built UFOs in the 1930's with the help of extraterrestrials.

There have been reported UFO sightings that are not alien spacecraft but are UFO's made by Earth people. They were experimental and we thought they were from outer space.

## Energy

Some of the information in this section appeared in various other sections.

Scalar energy has the potential to provide much of the world's energy needs and thus relieve humans of their dependency on fossil fuels. It will be much more possible in the future to use scalar energy as an effective healing modality.

Pyramids all around the world were built to create energy. That energy was not just for use on Earth but was also available for use in outer space as well as on Earth. The Great Pyramid at Giza was used as a hydrogen power plant to produce electrical energy.

Electricity can be broadcast wirelessly as Tesla thought.

The many ancient obelisks throughout the world were used for broadcasting electricity wirelessly. In 200 years we will transmit electricity wirelessly through the air on a large scale as Tesla tried to do. That technology was used in the time of the Atlanteans and before that.

It is possible that electric lights can be turned on without wires.

## New and future technology

Some of the information in this section appeared in *EVENTS OF THE FUTURE*

The technology exists for making cloaking devices to make objects appear invisible to the human eye.

It also exists for developing prosthetic gills for humans so that oxygen could be extracted directly from water for when they are underwater.

It will become economically viable to turn salt water into fresh water in the next fifty years.

The technology known as "the God Helmet" exists. It can transfer an individual's thoughts to another person. It cannot control another individual but it could put a thought into his mind without him knowing that it was not his own thought.

Although alchemists have tried for ages without success to transmute common elements into gold, the secret to doing so will be taken very seriously. The secret to making gold will be the mixing of different minerals.

Electro-magnetism will be used to counteract the force of gravity. It can be used on a wide scale to overcome gravity. We will be able to witness that somewhat but we will not be able to overcome gravity in our lifetime.

Stargates cannot be created through the use of technology.

The large Hadron Collider in Cern Switzerland will not present a potential serious danger to our planet.

Automobiles without wheels will run on our streets and highways in this century.

Airplanes and helicopters will have another engine for safety reasons.

There are ground vehicles with and without wheels on other planets. The wheel is an invention on all planets.

Flying cars will become more and more popular each year. Cars in the future will be able to fly and also be used as boats.

Within fifty years from now the majority of cars will not continue to use solely gasoline as power but will also use electricity and little fragments of oil, something that we are not aware of.

Within the next century there will there be a proliferation of robots that are practically indistinguishable from humans created by our technology. Some of those robots will be designed to serve as sexual partners for humans. They will look just like humans but will not be biological and will be very popular.

Robots will become our friends and they will be very useful in the future. In 380 years artificial humans will be virtually identical to biological humans. Women won't need men and likewise men won't need women.

It is not possible that robots of the future will have the ability to reproduce themselves.

Technology will reach the point where nearly all of the internal organs of humans could be replaced by mechanical means. A mechanical heart could be installed inside a person; a liver and other organs, too. The human brain can be replicated by mechanical means such as advanced computers or something similar.

Scientists will clone the bodies of human beings. They will be able to clone a human brain and place it in a cloned human body.

We will have the capability of transplanting the head of a person onto the body of another person as they have done with monkeys but it will not be successful. It is not possible to put the head of one species of animals onto the body of another species.

U.S. technology now has an unmanned space shuttle that has been in orbit for two years and is capable of disabling enemy satellites. What is already in space can disable satellites and satellites have already been disabled. The unmanned satellite affected the misfiring of North Korea's satellites. We are protecting ourselves through that satellite.

We now have remotely controlled flying drones which take photographs or move small objects from one place to another. That technology will develop to the point that it will be used on a widespread scale for moving people from one place to another.

Scientists will develop plasma beams so they can be used in a way similar to laser beams. That will be in our lifetime but it will not always be used for good.

The internet will continue to exist for many years to come but it will change radically from what it is now in our lifetime. The government will be taking increasing control over the internet and access will not be free.

There is technology for materializers like our 3D printers that can print 3D objects which can replicate objects such as UFO's and other large objects.

Within 50 years, mechanical robots will increasingly take over the functions of many activities that are now performed by humans to the point that human life will be very different from what it now is.

Gravity can be tapped to provide an endless source of energy. It is not necessary at this time that scientists be aware of how to provide an endless source of energy. It would create chaos and would disrupt the world economy if there were an endless source of energy.

Magnetism to create space travel at nearly the speed of light is secretly being used by our government. We will never find out all the things they are keeping from us.

Time travelling machines have been discovered periodically in several locations and then confiscated by our government. From the crash of the UFO in Roswell, New Mexico in 1947 a time machine was able to be reconstructed. The Nazis had a time machine that was shaped like our Liberty Bell.

Howard Hughes received information from extraterrestrials and his mental decline and demise was very much hastened by his enemies. He obtained the Tesla patents that were sequestered by the government and then gave them to George Van Tassel.

George Van Tassel built a time machine that was confiscated by the government.

We have the technology for time travel and the technology also exists for regressing a person from, for example, the age of forty to the age of twenty.

## Miscellaneous

Some of the information in this section appeared in various other sections.

Some of the crystals that the Atlanteans used to transmit energy are still in operation under the sea today in the area of the Bermuda Triangle and are the cause of the disappearance of planes and ships.

There are many more elements that have not yet been discovered by scientists.

Gold, silver and platinum are treasured in other star systems.

There is no truth to the theory that, because of modern technology, humans are being excessively bombarded with positive ions and this is having a negative effect on our health. Devices that are imbued with negative ions are of no benefit to our health.

The thoughts and feelings of humans have an effect on the properties of water. If there is a glass of water in front of us, our thoughts and feelings have an effect on the properties of the water and the effect can be measured.

At times there are conscious entities overseeing that what are considered to be the laws of science, such as the Law of Gravity, are implemented automatically whether by angels or other entities.

The German stealth aircraft existed during World War II but it was not successful.

There are subatomic particles smaller than quarks that we would call waves.

Major weather events, greater than just rain or snow, can be manipulated by the use of technology.

Humans have been taught that there are three states of matter: solids, liquids and gasses but now scientists say that there is fourth state called plasma. As the Theosophists believe, there are three additional subtle states of matter.

There is technology on Earth today that can destroy UFO's.

Since time and space do not actually exist, they are on the same continuum as some scientists speculate. There is a point where time becomes space and space becomes time. Time and space are fluid and flexible as proposed in Einstein's Theory of Relativity.

Our government has the technology that could replace fossil fuels, such as gas, oil and coal, as well as nuclear power for creating energy that could be used for electricity. That knowledge was gained from reversed engineering from the crashed UFO in 1947.

Our corporate and financial community has been powerful enough to keep that secret from government officials including the president.

Our government has a secret space program whose activities and achievements most people would find too incredible to believe.

As some scientists now believe, light can be created by using sound.

Nickola Tesla was able to create a UFO by discovering the key to overcome gravity.

Although the media have reported in the past few years that scientists have recently discovered planets around other stars, they have known about their existence for many years.

The more advanced a society is, the less they have need for technology. It is not necessarily true that the greater the technology, the more advanced society is; but in fact, the opposite is true.

# Part Two

# CHANNELED AND ADDITIONAL INFORMATION

# INTRODUCTION

I refer to the following passages as "inspired writings". I do not know if this information was channeled to me from an outside source or if it was channeled from my higher self. As these passages came to my mind, I could feel an abundance of energy that I could not explain. My thinking was certainly supercharged. I can neither identify the source nor can I vouch for the validity of what I say here. Nevertheless, the various concepts appear interesting and perhaps something worthy of consideration. I tried not to judge whether the concepts were appropriate, even those which seemed to run contrary to what I thought I knew. Sometimes the exact wording of statements would automatically appear in my mind. On the majority of occasions, the overall concept would come to mind. On those occasions I would write what came to mind and the writing would come very easily. Then as I would read what I had written, refinements would come to mind. Sometimes the thoughts came so fast that I missed them and was unable to write them down.

# CREATING YOUR PERSONAL BELIEF SYSTEM

Each person creates his own personal belief system regarding metaphysical or paranormal issues. For a great many people, religion does this for them by offering them a pre-packaged belief system. This package totally satisfies their needs by providing them with explanations of all they feel a need to know. Having faith in accepting what they are told is a significant element in providing them with comfort and security. If certain concepts are not part of the package, they can readily discard them.

Religion is vital to billions of people. Religion is important because it encourages positive behavior and consideration for those with whom we come into contact. Each religion is a pre-packaged belief system, some with little variation from others. Some are widely diverse, but all with the same core value that we refer to as the Golden Rule "Do unto others as you would have them do unto you."

Other people create their own belief system. In creating your personal belief system, imagine that you are making a large painting. The picture that you are painting is your belief system. This picture is in the form of a very large jigsaw puzzle. As you work on assembling the puzzle, initially you have no idea of what the final picture would look like. It is an ongoing lifelong paint-as-you-go project. There are a countless number of pieces. Each idea, fact, or concept is a piece of the puzzle. Not all pieces will end up being a part of the picture you are creating. Many of the pieces in front of you are beliefs that religions espouse. Some of those pieces will be used in your completed picture and some may not be part. Some pieces of the puzzle may run contrary to religious beliefs and may or may not be included in the picture you are creating.

As you examine each piece, you decide whether or not it is part of the picture you are creating. If you do not know if a particular piece is relevant to your picture or if you feel that it is not part of your picture, do not reject it. Simply put it aside and keep it in abeyance. As your picture takes shape, eventually you will know if the pieces that were put aside are part of the picture you are creating. The important thing is not to reject any piece until after your picture has been created. Only after the picture has been completed will you send pieces to the rubbish bin. Conversely as you are developing the picture, you may realize that some of the pieces you thought were part of the picture, were not really part of your picture after all.

The picture you have created is your own personal belief system. As you proceed in life you may meet other people who have created a picture that resembles yours in many ways to varying degrees. You may meet other people whose picture looks totally different from yours. The picture that each person creates is right for only that person. Always remember that belief systems are personal. It is not up to you to judge whether another person's system is right or wrong. Judge only your own belief system. Eventually you may realize that there is no universal belief system that is appropriate for everyone.

# THE EARTH IS NO LONGER FLAT

Many years ago I believed that the Earth was flat and that the sun and all the planets and stars revolved around the Earth.

Then as time went on, a few scientists made new inventions and were able to think outside of the box. They were able to show that the Earth was round and no longer the center of the universe.

There were even a few people who thought the scientists might be correct about this. I was one of the oddball believers in the round Earth theory but the Church absolutely forbade such beliefs. Unfortunately the Church wanted control and excommunicated me or maybe even executed me. Of course that was not in this lifetime.

Between that lifetime and this lifetime, the undisputable findings of science convinced the Church that the earth actually was round and was no longer flat. So it was not heresy anymore to openly say that the Earth was round and was not the center of the universe.

Yet some people continued to hold the traditional beliefs of the past and were unable to think that the Earth was not flat and not the center of the universe.

It is even likely that perhaps some people in the world of today are not ready to think outside of the box regarding the position of the Earth in the universe.

Now science is in the process of taking another step forward with speculation that intelligent life might exist on other planets throughout the universe, perhaps even more advanced life forms than the people of Earth.

Yet many people, if not most, adhere to the belief that extraterrestrial life is pure science fiction. Nevertheless, little by little, increasing numbers of people accept the speculation that perhaps intelligent life does exist elsewhere in the universe.

Just as in the past, when people adamantly held to the belief that the Earth was flat, most people today either hold to the belief that it is ridiculous to believe in the existence of alien life or at most hold to the belief that speculation of such thinking is reserved for off-the-wall kooks.

Taking a quantum leap into the abyss of insanity, there is even a small but slowly increasing percentage of people today who say they believe that extraterrestrials were and are instrumental in the creation and evolution of the human beings on Earth.

The great majority of us readily accept that God, or whatever name is given to the creative force, created all the vegetables and now Earth humans are grafting vegetables together or genetically modifying the vegetables in order to make them of more service to humankind. They feel they are making improvements on the work of the creator. It is like assuming the position of being a co-creator.

From that point of departure, it may not be an inconceivable leap of consciousness to envision God creating man and then extraterrestrials genetically modifying humankind to be of more service to them, just as we have done with vegetables. Extraterrestrials genetically modified Earth beings to the point that they created humans in their image. Perhaps that explains why the beginning of the book of Genesis in the Bible says, "Then God said, "Let <u>us</u> make mankind in <u>our</u> image, in <u>our</u> likeness."

# GOD AND PRAYER

There is much truth to the sayings, "As above, so below" and "As below, so above".

Our world and the worlds above us can be compared to a large corporation in which there are numerous levels of guidance, supervision and authority. Corporations can have many levels of bosses: advisors, managers, department heads, supervisors, vice-presidents, presidents, CEO's, all the way up to the Board of Directors.

As workers or employees, some of our wants, needs and problems can be satisfied at the level of our co-workers. After that they could be satisfied at the level of our bosses; such as our advisors, others at higher levels such as the department head. It is not at all uncommon for our wants and needs not to even reach the level of the CEO or the Board of Directors. The success of the corporation depends on the success of the bosses. The success of the bosses depends on the success of the lower level bosses. The success of the lower level bosses depends on the success of each individual worker.

Just as in this world, we can have different levels of bosses; there are different levels of "gods" above our world. What we consider these "gods" to be could actually be spirits, angels or even extraterrestrials and many others that we are unaware of. Even though there are many "gods", there is only one God. This God cannot be understood or explained at the human level, the spirit level or even levels above that. The concept of God is too far above that of what we might compare to the Board of Directors for the human mind to even begin to conceive or explain.

When we pray, we are expressing our requests, needs and desires. When we pray to God (whatever we may consider that may be), we are actually broadcasting our requests to all those levels (or heavens) above the physical realm. Our prayers are broadcast throughout creation. They can be responded to by beings in any of the levels above us. Thus, a variety of sources respond to our prayers; including those in the spirit world, the spirits of those in the physical world, the angels, and those in other realms as yet unknown to us.

Sometimes an entity in the spirit would be able to satisfy our needs. Other times a higher level entity such as an angel might be needed to respond to us. The level of potential assistance is inconceivable. An angel may assist a spirit in responding to our needs. A spirit may assist another human in helping us. All that is above our level is God. All that is at our level is God.

If we choose, we can select specific spirits to address our prayers to including those whom we revere and those to whom we have given the title of saints. We can call on angels but we should not call on them by name.

We often receive assistance from spirits and angels. They both have the ability to project thoughts into our minds. We don't usually realize that often our thoughts don't emanate from our own minds. Telepathic thoughts often appear as ideas that just seemed to pop into our heads. These thoughts can help us solve our problems or guide us in our actions.

The degree of telepathic assistance you receive is often related to the level of the entity to which you pray. You can call on your Aunt Becky who died many years ago. Depending on her level of evolution (what we often refer to as "spirituality") she may be able to help you. Spirits have different levels of energy (evolution) as do humans.

The role of angels is to help humans evolve to the God level for which they are destined. Angels can send helpful thoughts to your mind. They can also manipulate the laws of nature to help you. For example, they can prevent you from drowning when it appears that by all ordinary explanations you should have drowned. Evolved spirits and even some humans have the ability to manipulate the laws of nature. We refer to the manipulation of natural laws as "miracles."

Jesus the man (not Jesus the Christ) dwells in the spirit world. He is an extremely powerful spirit. His level of energy is so great that he can respond to all those who call upon him regardless of their religion. It does not matter what religion you practice. Jesus will help and guide you. There are others with very high energy level that can also help you if you call on them.

Our creator has set up the system of prayer to bring assistance to us, to guide us, and to bring comfort to us. Prayer is there for us to use. When, how, or whether to pray or is totally up to us. Prayer is not a requirement for humans. Many people are able to pass through life without tapping into the benefits of prayer. If they choose not to pray, God does not "punish" them.

Choosing not to take advantage of prayer can be compared to people traveling by automobile to a specific destination with no road signs or maps available to them and not having membership in the American Automobile Association for roadside assistance. If they choose to be on their own, that is there decision. They may eventually get to their destination but not without difficulties, trials and tribulations along the way. The solution is, "Make life easier and better for yourself. Take the easy way out. Pray."

# THE CARE OF THE EARTH

The earth is not being harmed by the actions of humans. The planet is far too advanced to allow itself to be harmed by humankind. However, the future of the human race is being altered by the actions of man. The altering of the future of Earth humanity is a definite future but can be delayed by the actions of man. Greater concern for the environment is a major factor in prolonging human life on Earth as it now exists. Nevertheless it is inevitable that major Earth changes will occur.

The earth is a very strong conscious entity, fully able to take care of itself as it has repeatedly done in the past when conditions were necessary for action to be taken. The earth must cleanse and renew itself, such as the event referred to as the Great Flood or in the destruction of Atlantis or Lemuria. It will continue to do this countless times in the future.

Perhaps, a parallel can be drawn between the earth renewing itself and a dog standing up and shaking itself to rid itself of fleas. Many fleas will be cast out but it is very likely that some will remain, and thus start the process of infestation over again. The dog will feel better for a while, at least until another shaking is necessary.

When the earth renews itself, a considerable portion of physical human life, if not all, will be destroyed just as it was in the time of Noah. The essence of human life, the soul, will not be destroyed, nor can it ever be destroyed. The physical body is simply a creation of the soul. Although some of these creations may remain after the earth restores itself, souls will remain as spirits but will not be able to reincarnate on Earth until conditions are appropriate for physical life on Earth again. Great numbers of souls will move on to the spirit worlds of different planets where their spirit form will abide. There they will again be able to reincarnate and continue to progress as if they had remained incarnate on Earth.

At the time of the earth's renewal, higher level extraterrestrial entities often come to the rescue of some Earth humans for preserving the continuance of the species for the future re-population of the new young earth. This has occurred numerous times the earth's ancient past and will occur numerous times in the earth's future. The Ascension of the earth from the third to the fourth density which is now occurring is instrumental to the process.

# THE BANQUET OF LIFE

It has been said that life is a sumptuous banquet that takes place in the most lavish of banquet halls. The dining room is impressively large and magnificently decorated, ornately appointed with plush carpeting, rich draperies, priceless works of art, and furnishings of great splendor. Throughout the hall are numerous elegantly carved dining tables surrounded by perfectly matched chairs. Each table is exquisitely set with delicate china trimmed in gold, drinking glasses of perfect crystal, beautifully crafted silverware and a variety of accouterments of such beauty that even the imagination of the beholder cannot exceed.

As we peer into the banquet hall, we easily note that the arrangement of tables has been designed with specific order. Near the entrance to the hall there are numerous tables around which are seated only people young of age. It is easy to note that these youth are filled with the lively anticipation of what is about to occur. They are so filled with the vibrancy of life and the excitement of the dining experience upon which they are about to embark. The conversation is animated and loud. They can be seen sitting on the edges of their chairs, hardly able to restrain their impetuousness, just waiting for the food to be served. For them, the wait seems endless; they are so anxious to begin.

The entire mid section of the banquet hall is filled with tables as far as one's vision can allow. Around these tables are seated many adults of their middle years of life. The meal has already been placed on the table. The numerous serving dishes are heaped with all kinds of delicious foods and there is an abundance of beverages of all varieties. The repast has begun and these guests are at various stages of the partaking of their meal. A full range of gustatorial sensations can be observed. They are filled, to varying degrees, with the pleasure of such heavenly enjoyment and it appears that nearly everyone wants the banquet to continue forever like this.

At the far end of the banquet hall, there are also many tables. Around these tables are seated only individuals who are beyond the years of the prime of life. They have finished their meal and look so satisfied and contented. Most of them are sitting back on their chairs with their arms crossed upon their chests. Although they no longer have the passion of the hunger they once had, they do have vivid memories of the experience and the feelings of enjoyment of partaking of the banquet.

As they delve back into their memories, many can even recall the time of the excitement of waiting for the food to be served when they were so hungry. As we look around at these tables, we can hear so many people saying as they lean back on their chairs, "My but that was a wonderful meal!" There are others who grimace as if such a thought gives them pain.

After finishing the meal, little by little each of them needs to rest for a while. So they go to a little door behind all the tables and go upstairs to regain their energy. After they have rested, some for a shorter period of time and others for a longer period of time, they go to another stairway above the entrance to the hall. They descend the stairway and arrive at the entrance to the hall. Once again they enter the banquet hall and are anxious to partake of another meal.

# IT'S NOT WHERE YOU END UP IN LIFE THAT COUNTS

In the latter years of life, some people live in the lap of luxury; enjoying life to the fullest extent, travelling wherever they want, doing whatever they want, having plenty of money to buy whatever their hearts desire. In spite of outward appearance, some may be content while others may be miserable. Some may be in good health and others in poor health. Some may have many friends, others with no friends.

There are other people who spend their life's final years living in poverty. Some are practically penniless, unable to procure even the necessities of life. They may even be in poor health and all alone with no one to share their lives with or even care for them. Their possessions are scant and insufficient for making life enjoyable. Just as with those living with all the trappings of life, some may be content while others may be miserable.

It seems that the majority of people spend the final years of their lives somewhere between those who live in luxury and those who live without the finer things of life.

Whether your latter years are spent in luxury, in poverty or somewhere between, it is of no importance to the real you; the you at the soul level. The important thing is what you did in life prior to your latter years. As we look at those around us in the latter years of life, we cannot observe their lifestyle to measure how successful they really are.

There are people who live in the lap of luxury in their latter years who are truly good souls whom we may admire. They have spent their lives being kind to others, helping whenever they could. In the process of living they gave little thought to their own welfare, but instead placed their focus on those who were in need. They lived by the golden rule.

Other people living in the lap of luxury in their final years are not to be admired. They have spent their lives selfishly, giving little thought to the hurt or harm they brought to others along the way of life's journey. All they cared about was themselves. Their mistreatment or lack of consideration of other people was their means of attaining what they desired and received.

Just as with those living luxuriously at life's end, so it is with those living at the opposite end of the scale. Some should be admired for their actions as they journeyed through life. Others should be pitied. The golden rule meant nothing to them.

Our lifestyles or our possessions are no part of our true selves. It is only what we are at the soul level that is of importance. No one can take lifestyles or possessions with them when they make their transition into the spirit world. They take only their actions with them, including what they have thought, said, or done. It is with their actions that they must live in the afterlife. It is the consequences of their actions that become the karma of their future lifetimes.

When all is said and done we cannot look at the lifestyles of older people and make any kind of judgment as to whether they are what we might call "good" people or what we might call "bad" people. It is not for us to determine if they are rich or poor in spirit.

# SOMETIMES THE ANSWER IS NO

Why doesn't God answer our prayers? We often have wants or needs that we pray and pray and pray for but God just doesn't listen to us. Sometimes our prayers are answered. On other occasions it seems that God just isn't listening. Why doesn't God always help us? Are there times that God is asleep? There are scriptures in the Bible that say "Ask and it shall be given." But we ask and it is not given. Have we proved that the Bible is wrong and is just not telling us the truth?

We often confuse our needs with our wants. We say, "I really need a larger screen television than the one I have." when we really mean, "I really want a larger screen television than the one I have." It is often difficult to distinguish our wants from our needs. We do not know the difference between the two.

Our desires come from our mind. Could it be that God just doesn't give us what we want because the mind of man is not the mind of God? God is universal and also personal; internal and external. That is, God rules the universe and has dominion over all that is, and yet God is within us. Our soul is our true self where God dwells.

A wise person once said that we pray to ourselves. We pray to our personal God, the God that is within us, the God that is part of us. It is our soul that knows what is best for us. If our wants or what we think are our needs run contrary to what is best for us, then we are protected when our prayers are not answered. We are saved from what could be disastrous for us. We must remember that sometimes unpleasantness or even tragedy in our lives is just what we need to point us in the direction that we should go.

We incarnate into the physical life to learn specific lessons so that we may advance in the evolution of our soul. If our wants prevent us from learning the lessons we need to learn, the God in our soul will protect us by not granting our wishes. Sometimes our life's lessons are of karmic origin. If, for example, we have shown extreme haughtiness toward others in previous lives, then it could be that humility is one of our lessons to learn in this lifetime. If we want something that will bring us the opposite of humility and cause to be haughty, then our wishes will not be granted. Our prayers will not be answered.

We must have faith in ourselves; that is, in the God that dwells in our soul. We must have faith and understand that we are provided with opportunities to advance in our spirituality when our prayers are not answered.

# WE ARE NOT ALONE

Although it may appear that when we are alone with no one else in our presence, we may think we are alone but in reality we are far from being alone. There is much more than just the physical world that we perceive through our senses. The non-physical world is very real and teeming with life, even more so that the physical world in which we live.

Every place in the universe is abundant with life, not physical life such as we humans but conscious entities that are invisible to us. This includes spirits, angels, animal spirits, elementals and many varieties of entities with which we are unfamiliar. Even our thoughts and the thoughts of others are a form of energy in the world that we cannot perceive through our five senses. Our thoughts populate the world around us. The thoughts of those in our presence are invisibly around us with a life of their own.

Our thoughts attract invisible entities around us. Good thoughts beckon beneficent beings. Negative thoughts attract negative beings. Our thoughts can attract assistance and guidance. Although we can do so, it is not necessary to pray for what we want. Just think it or better yet, visualize it. Do not underestimate the power of visualizing what we want.

We must never underestimate the power of our thoughts. Loving thoughts bring loving invisible energies. Hateful thoughts will bring negative energies that may even bring harm to us. We must be careful regarding the focus of our thoughts because the kinds of thoughts we have attract the type of energy that reflects the type of thoughts.

We can call upon spirits and we can call for angels for assistance. Think positive and we will get positive results. When we fear that the results will be negative, we will get negative results. Fear and doubt are our enemies.

Even when we see people around us, they are often not what they appear to be. Amongst us are extraterrestrials who are humans just like us and a few other extraterrestrials that appear totally different. Our neighbor may not be of origin on this planet. They often have abilities to monitor and access us that far exceed our power. Those from other star systems have abilities that are beyond that which we can even imagine. They can change their form and appearance at will. We refer to them as shape shifters. This is for real.

# OUR THOUGHTS AND TELEPATHY

A major part of the work of the spirits is to help and protect humans. Every person receives guidance and assistance from individuals in the spirit world. The majority of us are not even aware that we are guided by the spirits.

Very often communication from spirit guides comes as intuition or "thoughts from out of the blue". We often give ourselves credit for being so intelligent, so clever or so perceptive when actually the origin of our ideas was not from our own mind.

Each of us has a spirit guide that stays with us from the time we are born until the time we die. Some people have more than one guide. At times other spirits come to help us in specific situations.

Even though most people are oblivious to their spirit guide, there are some people, such as Sondra had, who have the ability to hear and communicate directly with their guide.

Most of the time, I don't know the origin of many of my thoughts. I don't always know if they emanate from my own mind or if they are received telepathically.

Telepathy is an activity performed not only by spirits but by humans as well. Our thoughts are energy; energy that is projected throughout the universe, never stopping. Anybody can pick up on them. For example, it is not at all uncommon to think about a person and then sometime shortly afterward that person calls you on the phone or you run into him at the supermarket.

The US patent office is filled with examples of people who almost simultaneously applied for a patent on the same idea. Alexandra Graham Bell is credited with having invented the telephone but it was actually Elisha Gray who applied for the patent first but a snafu at the office caused the patent to be granted to Bell instead.

Those in the spirit world are at a higher level of vision than those in the physical world. This means that spirits have the natural ability to see and understand more than humans do. They can see what we can do to improve our lives, what can be done to solve our problems and what lies ahead for us. The intent, goal or purpose of the high level spirits is to help humanity, individual by individual, so that all mankind can evolve to higher levels in their spiritual evolution.

Like Sondra, there are people in our world who can communicate with their guide and often able to share information that they receive from their guide to help other people.

# THE HIGHER SELF

The higher self has been defined as "the elements and aspects of the soul that are essential to the current incarnation". It is the deepest level of an individual's consciousness that can be accessed by the individual.

All humans and humanoids throughout the universe are manifestations of the soul and have the level of consciousness referred to as the higher self.

All entities channel their higher selves to varying degrees but all are not aware of doing so. Since some souls are more evolved than others, the validity of the extent and accuracy of the channeling of the higher self varies accordingly. Therefore, the channeled messages of some people are more accurate than that of others.

I am able to access my higher self through the use of the pendulum, as are millions of people through the world. Due to the level of my evolution and my proficiency with the pendulum, my channelings are very accurate.

Eventually I will no longer need the pendulum to access my higher self and will then be a psychic, as was Sondra. Just as all souls are not equal in their evolution and, consequently, the level of their higher self, all psychics are not equal in their ability to channel extensive and accurate information when they provide their readings.

Psychics and pendulum users are able to provide information about other people because the higher selves of all people are connected.

I now realize that I was channeling my higher self when I said that my thinking was supercharged. I was not channeling another entity.

# FREE WILL AND PREDICTIONS

One of the attributes of human beings is free will. The exercise of a person's free will is the faculty that enables them to make decisions. Their will is what gives them the ability to have desires; although conditions may be such that they cannot follow through on their desires, such as actions imposed by other people (being in jail, for example).

Their desires determine how people react in situations or to stimuli. Predicted actions of a person can only be based on how they have responded to similar situations or stimuli in the past. It is like feeding a lot of information into a computer and then having the computer arrive at an outcome; for example, how the stock market will react to what occurs, the Kentucky Derby odds etc.

Donald Trump was predicted to be reelected but he screwed up by some of the decisions he made. He would have been reelected. Since he had free will, no one could predict his actions with absolute certainty and the consequences of actions that weren't predicted. Psychics and mediums (those who receive information from the spirits) cannot always predict the future with 100 percent accuracy when the exercise of a person's free will is involved.

# UNDERSTANDING GOD

There are no words in our language or in any other language that can even begin to explain what God is. In order to have a minimal understanding of God, we have brought the concept of God down to our level of thinking. Since humans are physical beings, we have likened God unto a physical being like ourselves in order to understand God. Even when compared to spirits and angels, the abilities of humans are severely restricted. Thus, we put limitations on what God is when we define God as a product of our thinking. In all aspects God is limitless. Our human minds cannot even comprehend the concept of "limitless". Whether it is space, time, or abilities, we cannot conceive "limitless" as having no beginning or no end.

Civilizations throughout history have tried to grasp an understanding of God. To do this, it has been necessary to define God in the only terms we know, human terms.

The Bible says that God created man in God's image. The Bible also says, although somewhat indirectly, that man created God in man's image. There are dozens of passages that mention the hand of God. For example, one verse says, "But to which of the angels he said, 'Sit on my right hand, until I make thine enemies my footstool." Apparently if God has a right side God must also have a left side.

If God uses a footstool God must have feet. Moses saw the backside of God. The heart of God and the Godhead are also mentioned. God has a throne that God sits on, so God must have another body part. To the best of my knowledge, nothing is mentioned about God having fingers, toes or hair or even a long white beard.

We know that God is male rather than female because the Bible refers to God as He. God also procreates because he has sons and daughters. The minds of humans are so limited that they cannot even begin to conceive the concept of God.

Even the use of pronouns (He, His and Him) to refer to God is human thinking. Instead of "He" or "Him" we might better say "God". Instead of "His", we might better say "God's".

God is essentially neutral, impartial in his treatment of people. No favoritism. None are in disfavor. Everything takes place in accord with the spiritual laws that have been established. God does not choose us. It is we who choose God. We tend to interpret the implementation of the law of karma as God's showing favoritism or punishment to us.

Just as there are physical laws, there are spiritual laws. Some laws we must abide by; such as gravity in the physical world and karma in the spiritual. Other laws are principles that are ours to use if we choose. We may choose not to use electricity. We can get by without electricity. We may choose not to use prayer. We can get by without it. In either case, we are limiting ourselves and making our lives more difficult.

# THE INCONCEIVABILE HUMAN PROGRESSION

Humans evolve through seven levels, sometimes referred to as seven heavens; the seventh being the highest of all. When we reach the seventh heaven, we are at the God level.

At that level we become God. We become the god of a whole new universe. As a god, we then also evolve through seven levels, much higher than the previous seven levels through which we evolved.

When we then arrive at the seventh heaven, we are at a new God level. We become God again, much more evolved than the previous god level. We are the god of a new universe, much higher than the previous universe for which we were the god.

This process repeats itself over and over. Higher level gods are repeatedly being created. Just as time and space are endless, without beginning or end, so it is with the evolution of all of creation. There is no limit on the level of evolution of all that is.

Is this what the Bible means when it says that we are the children of God? As children, why shouldn't we grow up to the point that we are like our parent?

# LEARNING TO GET TO BE WHERE YOU WANT TO BE IN LIFE

All of us, except perhaps a very small percentage who are among the more enlightened souls, have very immutable preconceived notions about ourselves. Sometimes others view specific aspects of our personality in accord with our own views. More often than not, however, those who know us well see us quite differently from the way we perceive ourselves.

Considering that there are numerous aspects of our personality, the closer our views of specific aspects of our personalities are to the views of others, the more real understanding we actually have of ourselves. It is quite likely that if you ask others if they understand themselves, most in all sincerity will respond, "Yes, very well." In most instances, this answer couldn't be further from the truth.

The closer our views of the various aspects of our personality are to the views of those who know us well, the greater the potential we will have for a truly successful, happy and fruitful life. The comparison must be made by those who know us well, certainly not by strangers we meet or even by those we do not actually know very well.

A person may view himself as being a very interesting conversationalist, for example, because of the amusing anecdotes or stories he relates. Others who are not well acquainted him may find him very entertaining. On the other hand, those who know him well may find him very boring because he keeps repeating the same stories over and over again. There are always exceptions; it could be that a few of those who know him well enjoy hearing the same stories repeatedly.

If you learn to see yourself as most others see you and then make changes to be in accord with how they see you, it is more likely that they will have a better opinion of you and will treat you in a more positive manner. If you feel that you are a very cheerful person, try to discover if others feel the same about you. You might discover that most others see you as a very grumpy, complaining person. That could be a learning point; a point where you could make changes to improve your relations with others.

Think about the following statements you could say about yourself and then seek to see if others would agree with you:

I have a wonderful sense of humor.

I am reliable and you can always depend on me.

People don't like me because I am short and fat.

I am sincere and honest.

I am really sexy and good looking.

I treat others very politely and with respect.

People don't like me because I am ugly.

I pay careful attention to time and always arrive on time.

I am not a controlling person.

I am not hot tempered or argumentative.

My way is the best way.

I have good common sense.

I shouldn't smile because my teeth look bad.

I treat everyone equally.

I do not have an attitude of superiority.

I am a very humble person.

Everybody loves me.

I am an easy going person and easy to get along with.

I am always open to new ideas.

I am not stubborn or closed minded.

I am a good listener.

I speak well and with clarity.

I am not a boring person.

I always treat others politely and with respect.

Etc.

If anyone says something about you that runs contrary to the way you feel about yourself ("You're such a snob."), don't just brush it off. Consider the possibility that there might be some truth in it. The above mentioned are but a few of the many possibilities of how we might consider ourselves and adjust our thinking and behavioral patterns accordingly.

# THE PLACEBO EFFECT ON HEALING

When pharmaceutical companies are testing the effects of a new medicine they often have a trial study done with the new medicine and an inert compound called a placebo. Theoretically there could be four kinds of patient groups:

1. Those that were given the placebo but were told that they were given the new medicine.

2. Those that were told that what they were given might be the new medicine or might be a placebo.

3. Those that were told that what they were given a placebo.

4. Those that were told that they were not given a placebo, but the actual medicine

Studies would show that the healing effect of the placebo was most positive for those in group one, less effective for those in group two, and rarely if ever effective for those in group three. The more faith the patient has in the procedures the greater the possible healing effect.

A similar effect occurs with what we might hands-on or energy healers. Many healers simply place their hands on the patient or simply tell them that they are sending healing energy to them. This is often an effective healing modality.

Other healers increase the patient's faith in the process by establishing healing rituals. The routines vary from healer to healer.

Sometimes the routines can be very simple, for example having the patient just repeat a few words or sentences that the healer speaks or by using mantras.

Sometimes the routines can be more complex by having the patient perform certain tasks. The healing effects increase with the complexity of the tasks that must be performed. Even fraudulent healers can have the ability to heal, often when they require the patient to pay them for their services.

Although the healing stimulus may be external, the reality is that we heal ourselves by energizing the healing ability within us.

# THE LOOP OF INFINITY

Time is the loop of infinity, with neither beginning nor end. It just goes on and on. The future is the past. The past is the future. Time continually renews itself. The loop of infinity never ends, always renewing and repeating itself. Repetition is renewal, the loop of eternity. Just like time, space is also infinite. It loops around and repeats itself; no beginning, no end. Time and space blend with energy. Energy exists on the framework of time and space. Energy renews itself continuously. It is endless and vibrant forever.

Time and space ride on the back of energy. It is eternal action without beginning or end. Energy is just a single action. A single action is all actions. All actions are a single action, just as time is a single point and space is a single point. Space can be in fragments and time can be fragmented. Yet they cannot be separated from the whole. Nothing exists except for the loop of infinity of time, space and energy. Time, space and energy flow in all directions. They are all one. All that exists is one.

# EXTRATERRESTRIALS AND THE PRESENT-DAY WORLD

The following passage consists of excerpts taken from the channeling sessions presented by the spirit guide to my wife Sondra. They are a compilation of remarks made by the spirit guide. The following passages are in the words of the spirit guide.

Even though many of you may think that extraterrestrials are the work of science fiction, I assure you that we are indeed real. Since the beginning of time on your planet we have played a very significant role in both the development of your planet and the development and evolution of mankind.

We are much more highly evolved than Earth humans and are assisting them to elevate their level of achievement. We have far greater mental capacities and abilities than you Earth people have. Earth humans use only a small portion of their brains. Those on other planets use a much greater percentage of their brains. We can communicate using telepathy. We can create objects and conditions simply with our minds.

Although Earth humans are the least evolved of all human life on the various planets, they are evolving to be more like us. With the forthcoming Ascension or, as some say, the movement from the third density to the fourth density, humanity will be much different than it is now.

There are thousands of different species of extraterrestrials. All of us have a humanoid form; a torso, a head, two arms and two legs. The great majority of extraterrestrials look exactly like Earth people. Although not all are of a benevolent nature to humans, nearly all of them are here to assist you. Since the very beginning of life on Earth, extraterrestrials have been, and still are, on your Earth.

The current social and political situation in your country and worldwide had its roots eons ago, even before Biblical times and that of Atlantis. It is addressed in your Bible and in the scriptures of many religions. It is a necessary part of the Ascension of mankind. It is the struggle between good forces and evil forces.

It began as the struggle between opposing extraterrestrial groups, the Luciferians and the Elohim, what you now refer to as the Cabal and the Alliance. Conditions are not always what they appear to be. Until you have attained the power of discernment, make no judgments about what you see or hear. Remember but do not judge.

At the current time, evil forces have become energized but they will be defeated by the forces for the good of humanity. Even after defeat, evil will once again eventually raise its head and confront the good. The good will always eventually defeat the evil.

# UNUSUAL EVENTS AFTER I MET SONDRA

Several unusual experiences occurred shortly after I met Sondra before we became husband and wife. This first thing I noticed was that I was experiencing what I called "burning". This went on for several weeks. It was like when you spend the day on the beach and then at night in bed your body seems on fire just exuding heat.

Sondra was a medium and a psychic who was very sensitive. When she would touch me, she could feel my skin vibrating. There were occasions that I touch her on the forehead she practically passed out. After a few weeks, the "burning:" stopped. For years I had no explanation for this happening. Then I realized that vibrations cause heat. Years later Sondra's spirit guide explained that my vibrational level was being raised to meet her level.

Another rather unusual experience before we were married occurred when I was shopping at the local supermarket. As I was walking down an aisle, I felt as though gravity was no longer having the normal effect on me and that I was becoming weightless. This was not a pleasant sensation.

Perhaps the strangest occurrence before we were married was when I took a friend to her home for a reading. After the reading we sat around for hours talking. It was well past midnight when Sondra said that she saw Mahatma Gandhi sitting cross-legged in a white robe next to me. He told her that he was my friend. I had no idea why he chose to be there with me.

Although I am not able to explain the intensity of what next occurred in words, I felt his mind or some part of his spirit enter my body. I could sense his feelings. It was almost as if we were one. He felt that it was so good to have physical sensations again. At the time, I remember touching my right hand back and forth on my left arm and sensing his feelings rather than my own. At the same time, I did not feel as though I was touching my own arm. He was enjoying the opportunity of physical sensations. After a short time, he left.

In the years that followed, Gandhi did come through to Sondra several times. The pendulum has told me that Sondra was mistaken in that it was not Gandhi but rather her own spirit guide. The pendulum has also told me that Gandhi has no connection with me.

# ONE- LINERS

The more you give, more you get.

It's not how far you progress. It's how much you progress.

You don't need religion. You just need the golden rule.

You must earn love before you can learn to love.

When your memory goes, you are forced to live in the now.

Losing your memory of past events gives you the freedom from being tied down to them.

Stupidity is not a virtue; neither is ignorance.

I honor myself when I am of assistance to (i.e. show respect for)

others .

The greatest burden that people carry on their shoulders is their past.

Try radiating positivity.

Death is not a bad thing for those who die. It is a bad thing only for those who remain behind.

The best way to show your gratitude for the assistance you receive from God is to be of assistance to other people.

Why doesn't God answer my prayers? Every day I pray to God for patience and that God give it to me immediately.

If you do not undertake adventures in your life, then you are a candidate for the undertaker.

If I have so many aches and pains at age 80, how did Methuselah feel at age 969?

How do we recognize the difference between intuition and ego mind chatter?

Whenever you use any of your senses you can see the true beauty. It brings the soul higher to God.

Being in the light is greater than seeing the light.

Success in life is measured in terms of what you take with you when you die.

Life is what happens while you're waiting for something to happen.

Love is the realization of the feeling of oneness with all that is.

We each etch our niche in time and so we carve our place in history.

When I forgive, I relieve myself of the burden of unneeded weight on my shoulders.

# ON THE HUMOROUS SIDE

In regard to chocolate, Sondra and I had a little problem. She liked milk chocolate and I preferred bitter sweet dark chocolate. After considerable discussion, sometimes quite animated, we arrived at a crisis-preventing solution. We should only have milk chocolate. I truly admired Sondra for being so skilled in changing my mind.

As a medium Sondra would often talk in her sleep. Sometimes I didn't know if she was talking to a spirit or to me.

I once heard her say, "I really love my husband but I'm too tired to tell him that. You tell him."

We often had three-way conversations in bed at night. Sondra was talking to me and then also to someone else in the middle of our conversation, someone I could not hear. I wished I could have heard the other side of the conversation so I wouldn't have felt left out.

On several occasions Sondra spoke in Tongues in her sleep.

I once overheard Sondra tell someone that we have five bathrooms in our house but complained that I only let her use one at a time.

Quoting Sondra: "Don't ask me what I meant by that, I just said it."

# ON THE HUMOROUS SIDE

# Part Three
# SONDRA

# CONTACT WITH SONDRA AFTER HER DEATH

Sondra made her transition to the spirit world in April 2020 but it wasn't until June 2021 that contact was made with her.

One day the thought came to me that I should try using my pendulum to answer some questions about my life, even though I had not really seriously used the pendulum before.

I began asking the pendulum all kinds of questions and received plausible responses. On several occasions when I was asking questions, the pendulum became very erratic when giving answers. I knew that this was something that spirits could do because the pendulum was the easiest object for spirits to move since it required the least amount of their energy to make anything move.

When the erratic movements would occur, I would simply say, "Please go away in peace because I want to use my pendulum". They would always go away when I said that. Then one day when the pendulum was acting erratically, I asked the pendulum if a spirit that I knew was trying to contact me and the response was "yes".

When I then asked if it was a family member, it responded "yes". When I asked if it was my mother, it responded "no". When I asked if it was Sondra, the response was "yes". Then I said, "Is that you Sondra?" The response was "yes". After a few questions, I learned that Sondra had been trying to contact me almost immediately after she had died.

She had also been trying to get my attention by making things in the house disappear. The most notable was when she made my shoes disappear for about a week. When I searched for them everywhere in the house I could not find them. Then one day I was walking past the armchair on which I often sat and there they were, right where I had left them. They were in a very obvious place and had not been there when I had previously looked at that place on several occasions.

It was interesting to note that when I asked the pendulum where the lost things were, the pendulum gave me all wrong answers, which sent me on a wild goose chase all over the house. That was because they were not in the house but they should have been. Sondra also tried to get my attention by causing the numbers on the digital clock in the bedroom to shimmer and to move about on several occasions.

One day in June 2021, I invited three knowledgeable friends to my home to witness Sondra's responses to several questions I had prepared in advance. I also asked them to ask her questions while

I held the pendulum.

The questions and responses are as follows. All of the questions were answered "yes" except those followed by (No).

Would you answer some questions about how you experienced dying and going to where you are now?

Did you feel any more physical pain after you died? No

Did you feel any emotional pain after you died?

Were you immediately aware that you had died?

Did you have any feelings right after you died?

Were you trying to keep alive until I woke up so that I could be with you when you died?

As soon as you died, did you see your body and the surroundings in the room?

Could you see me give you my final kiss good-by when I tried to give you artificial resuscitation?

Were you aware of everything that was taking place when the 911 people were here?

Were you frightened or confused? No

Did you know what you should do after you died?

Did you see a white light?

Did you see a kind of tunnel?

Did you immediately go into the light and then the tunnel?

Did you wait a while before doing anything? No

Was getting into the spirit world difficult? No

Did everything you saw seem as real as they appeared when you were alive?

Did they appear more real?

Did you feel comfortable when you got into the spirit world?

As soon as you got into the spirit world, were people there to meet you?

Was your guide there, your family and friends?

Was our dog Lady there?

Were there family members that you did not know?

Did you communicate to each other by speaking? No

Did you communicate to each other by some kind of telepathy?

Were you at the gravesite burial service with us?

Did you hear *Somewhere Over the Rainbow* [as you had said you wanted at your funeral]?

Was just a coincidence that the woman had that

song on her phone so she could play it then? No

Do you feel that you have become accustomed to being where you are now?

Do you enjoy being there?

Can you create whatever you want by using just your mind?

Have you recreated anything that the two of us had together when we were here?

Does that make you feel more comfortable, more at home where you are?

Did you recreate our house, yard, our favorite car the Rolls Royce that was stolen?

Did you also create other things?

Do you know if anyone else there can see those things? No

Did you try to get in touch with me shortly after you arrived there?

Was it you who telepathically gave me the idea of using the pendulum?

Did I frustrate you because I didn't even realize that you were trying to do so?

Have you contacted anyone else since you have been there?

Have you been working with others there?

Have you been receiving help or advice from others?

Have learned anything or made progress since you arrived there?

Are you able to somehow know what is going on in our world?

Are you able to visually see things and hear things? No

Do you just sense what is going on?

When you arrived where you are, did you have any kind of review or flash backs of events in your lifetime here?

Are there different colors than there were on Earth?

Are there different kinds of sounds and music there?

Are you happier than where you ever were in the physical world?

Are you looking forward to me coming over when I get there?

Will you still have that big wall clock that I asked you to have for me when I get there?

Will it still not have any hands on it when I get there?

Are you able to choose whatever physical age you want to show to other spirits?

Are you able to show yourself as you were in other lifetimes? No

In the future will you be able to do that?

Was the lifetime you just had was your strongest lifetime? No

Did you have stronger lifetimes prior to this lifetime?

Do you understand why you had Multiple Sclerosis?

Do you still feel that your mother was the cause of your MS? No

Do you feel that your mother was just simply the instrument to bring on your MS and that she was really a good friend?

Do you feel that your mother loves you even though she acted as if she didn't love you in life?

Do you feel that you are not yet at the level of evolution that you no longer have the need for further incarnations?

Do you look forward to me coming there and being with you?

Do you see us being reincarnated together again?

Do you see me being reincarnated on another planet?

Do you see us together many more times in the spirit world?

Do you feel more knowledgeable now than you did when you were on Earth?

Would you advise people to look forward to the time when they cross over?

Was crossing over any kind of problem or difficulty for you? No

Was crossing over easy for you?

Have you seen Sid [her first husband of 32 years] since you crossed over?

Do you feel that you still have the same relationship with Sid that you had him? No

Do you feel that Sid is no longer your husband?

Do you I feel that we are still married?

Do you have relationships there? No

Do you have friendships that you might call companionships there?

Are you able to become aware of the past thoughts and actions of people?

Can you see scenes from when you were here, such as your home as it was when you were a child?

Could go back in time and actually be at your home and move around in it as it was then?

Could you witness or re-experience past events such as our wedding ceremony?

Do you have a greater degree of patience than when you were here?

Are you able to predict the timing of future events? No

Is that because time does not exist in your world and cannot be measured?

Can you recall events of your lifetime with me more vividly and with greater clarity than you could then?

Can you recall events from other previous lifetimes?

Are you interested in recalling events of past lives?

Can you see whatever you want to see?

Do you perceive spirits by their energy rather than by their physical form?

Would you agree with your guide when he said that spirits are energy beings rather than physical beings?

Have you noticed that some spirits always have more energy than other spirits?

Do you sometimes need to rest in order to restore your energy?

Do you use up your energy when you help others?

Can you instantaneously be in the presence of or be in contact with other spirits?

Can you communicate simultaneously with more than one spirit on totally different matters?

Can you do that with more than three?

Can you be in more than one place at the same time?

Can you be in different time periods simultaneously?

Is it easier for you to show yourself to some people than it is for you to show yourself to other people?

Does that mean that you have to use more energy to show yourself to some than to others?

Have you tried to show yourself to me?

Were you unsuccessful in doing so because I subconsciously block the appearance of spirits?

Maria and Carolina said they saw you when I was asking you questions. Did you show yourself to them?

Was that easy for you because they are very perceptive?

Have you visited other places throughout the universe?

Can you see and understand yourself more accurately than when you were alive?

Could you read the minds of humans as soon you crossed over?

Have you communicated or shown yourself to people other than Maria, Carolina or myself? No

Do you know if it is easier to communicate with people at nighttime? No

Is that because you haven't tried?

Do you look forward to when I communicate with you?

Do you feel it is true that Lillian Henry had a great impact on my life even though I haven't seen her since I was 13 years old?

Were you impressed with her and are of like minds and will be friends with her?

Are my mother and you close friends?

Can you read other spirits' minds without using your five senses?

Do you have the same five senses but they use them in a different way from the way we do?

# FROM SONDRA

Although my wife Sondra is no longer in the physical world, as part of her legacy she left behind some interesting writings, some of which are included a previous publication, *Glimpses from Beyond.*

# AN EXPLANATION OF MY CHANNELING

For me, channeling information from unseen sources is a very natural process. It has always been part of my life on this earth. I receive both psychic and channeled information. By this, I mean that thoughts, ideas, pictures, symbols, feelings, hunches etc. just come into my mind, often when I am thinking about a particular topic but also often when my conscious thoughts are unrelated to the information received.

Perhaps this information does come from an unseen outside source (that is, channeled) but I sense a difference between psychic and channeled information. I feel that psychic information comes from my higher self at the soul level or from a source that is not related to specific entities that channel information to me. This I feel but I do not know, nor can I explain the difference.

I do, however, sense four different ways of receiving information from outside sources that I channel. The first is that ideas just flow into my mind. These are not words, but rather concepts that I can easily convert into conscious speech. As I relax, the words flow very easily from my mouth. I sense a difference that I am unable to explain between receiving information through this modality and receiving information psychically.

The second way I receive information is that I actually hear someone speaking inside my head; words that I could repeat aloud if I so choose. I often have to pay careful attention because my mind must keep up with the pace of the voice of the speaker. If I am distracted or do not pay careful attention, the words are not repeated by the sender but are lost to me. This can, on occasion, be quite disconcerting. There could be gaps in what I hear or the information is so abundant that my memory cannot recall all that was said.

The third means of receiving information is when I am in an altered state and allow the channeler to speak through me. Although it appears that my consciousness is not in this dimension, it seems that both my awareness of this world and the voice of the speaker are inside my head. Although the channeler is speaking through me, I have the ability to censor, block or alter what comes out of my mouth. When I return to this reality, I am able to remember only certain parts of what I spoke aloud.

The fourth means of channeling, which I call deep-trance channeling, is when my consciousness appears to be fully dormant. I am speaking aloud but I am totally unaware of what I am saying and have no ability to control what I say. After channeling, I come slowly back to my everyday third dimension level of consciousness and have no memory or only foggy memories of what was said through me.

# SPIRIT GUIDES

Every person receives guidance and assistance from individuals in the spirit world. The majority of us are not even aware that we are guided by the spirits. Very often communication from spirit guides comes as intuition or "thoughts from out of the blue". We often give ourselves credit for being so intelligent, so clever or so perceptive when actually the origin of our ideas was not from our own mind.

Both spirits and angels have the ability to communicate with us telepathically. That is, they can project thoughts or ideas into our minds. How we respond to those thoughts or ideas is totally up to us. This is because each human has been endowed with a free will. We are the masters of our own fate.

Each of us has at least one spirit guide that stays with us from the time we are born until the time we die. Some people have more than one guide. At times other spirits come to help us in specific situations.

Even though most people are oblivious to their spirit guide, there are some people, however, who have the ability to hear and communicate directly with their guide.

Those in the spirit world are at a higher level than those in the physical world. This means that spirits have the natural ability to see and understand more than humans do. They can see what we can do to improve our lives, what can be done to solve our problems and what lies ahead for us.

The intent, goal or purpose of the high-level spirits is to help humanity, individual by individual, so that all humankind can evolve to higher levels in their spiritual evolution.

There are people in our world that can communicate with their guide and are often able to share information that they receive from their guide to help other people.

# MY SPIRIT GUIDE

My guide is a very old soul; that is, he has had many, many incarnations in the physical both on Earth and in other star systems. He states that the earth is not his home base. We may therefore assume that he is of extraterrestrial origin. He views life in the physical as very difficult and says that he has no desire to reincarnate.

He does at times, at his discretion, manifest himself to me visually also but not always. He has told me that he can manifest himself to me in whichever of his incarnation experiences he chooses. He has said he does not come to me in the visual form of his last lifetime but rather when he was on Earth in Biblical times.

He appears as a prominent personage in the Old Testament of the Bible. It is his preference to show himself as an old man with a white beard, dressed in a robe, wearing sandals and holding a crook in one of his hands; often walking on sand such as a beach or on cobblestones.

A few times he has shown himself to me as a younger, strong, muscular healthy man. I do not know if that was his younger self in his Biblical lifetime or if it was he in another incarnation. I know nothing else of his other lives in the physical. He told me his name as a Biblical personality.

Actually, since I am not well versed in Biblical characters, his identity was of little significance to me. Practically all I know about his life as portrayed in the Bible was told to me by my husband, who had a strong religious upbringing. He did indeed play a significant role in the Bible.

Since spirits have distinct personality characteristics just as do humans, I will attempt to tell you what I know about his personality. He is a gentle soul, kind and caring. He has quite a sense of humor, which can often be misinterpreted as what we might call a big ego. Yet he is modest and unassuming. He takes pleasure in helping those on our plateau. I say "others" because he has told me that he is the guide for other people in addition to me. He is quite down to earth and at times can be even rather earthy, even having a sharp tongue.

When I am communicating with him, I often question what he tells me and I dispute what I am told. When I am in the third form of channeling, as described in the previous section, I sometimes hold back and do not say aloud what he tells me, or I tone down what he says to make it sound more dignified or tactful.

I sometimes cover up his earthiness. It seems that tact takes a backseat to truth in the information my guide provides. There is something almost like a childlike honesty in his communication.

He has told me that English is not his language and that on rare occasions it is difficult for him to understand what we are saying to him. To us his spoken English is quite good. His vocabulary is rather extensive and his speech is precise although his phraseology is sometimes slightly different from what we might use, almost bordering what one might think of as slightly old-fashioned.

For example, he would often say "'tis" instead of "it's" or in answering a question that would evoke a "yes" answer, he would say "indeed" to mean "yes". He often says, "They are existing" rather than "They exist".

Many people have told me that they particularly enjoy his down-to-earth type of speaking rather than the inspirational or lofty platitudes that are often channeled through other mediums.

When someone once asked him a question in English but with a thick foreign accent, my guide asked him to ask his question in Spanish, the questioner's native language. The man then asked the question in Spanish and the guide answered in English through me.

I myself do not comprehend Spanish at all but his response was very clear to the questioner. The guide has also answered questions asked in Portuguese, Italian, Polish and Russian.

When I asked him what language he was most comfortable speaking, my guide's response was "Tongues". He says that Tongues is a fantastic way of expressing oneself. It is something that is built into the system of everyone who has a brain.

It is interesting to note that some of what I know about him did not come from what he said to me or how I visually perceived him. Instead, it came from what members of our group told me after I had concluded a deep-trance channeling session.

Although I knew he liked me, it made me feel good to hear group members repeat all the nice things he said about me and some of my specific traits that he liked. When I would channel, he would refer to me as "she" or "her" but never by my name.

Using my name could have pulled me back into this reality. The group enjoyed my disputing him and his earthiness. His sense of humor often evoked laughter from the group.

We can make a parallel if we assume that all Earth people are in the second grade in school. To us the whole school is our teacher. Our teacher is the whole school. We cannot conceptualize beyond that. Some students are more intelligent and some are less intelligent. If we need help, we can ask a more intelligent classmate.

Sometimes more intelligent students know the answers to your questions. Sometimes they do not. Even the more intelligent students can sometimes give you the wrong answers. We seek help from all our classmates.

Then one day, a high school student enters our classroom and says he will help us with our work. To those of us in the second grade, the high school student appears as an intellectual giant who knows everything.

We do not consider that there are others above the level of a high school student who knows more than he knows. All we know is that we have in our presence someone who can immediately assist us. Perhaps we are the second graders and the guide is the high school student.

In addition to my guide, I sometimes allow others from the astral world to speak through me. Years ago, when I would deep-trance channel in front of a group, my listeners told me that I was speaking in a thick Irish brogue. I have often been told that there are very slight but perceptible facial changes when I channel certain entities.

For more information about interesting experiences with other non-physical entities, I suggest you read my first book Scattered Glimpses: A Mosaic.

# CHANNELED POETRY

I have explained that, as a psychic, thoughts come to me in different ways: I see mental pictures; I just know things; I hear voices saying specific words; Ideas just come into my head. Although I wish I could, I cannot always explain how I receive things.

Several years ago, even before I thought of writing a book, when I was feeling especially sorry for myself, lines started coming to me. They were not channeled in my regular way, but instead I would hear a voice in my head dictate the lines and I would just write them down.

It was like someone else, in the background, was supercharging my thinking. Sure, I was doing the thinking, but my mind couldn't keep up with the pace of my thoughts. Sometimes even poetry, it seemed, came to me from out of nowhere.

I had channeled poetry before but this was different. I was writing it, but yet I wasn't writing it. I probably sound off the wall at this point, yet I know I am not. One thing I was never able to do was to write poetry. In all my years of formal schooling, this was one thing at which I did anything but excel. Now all of the sudden, there I was, writing poetry with the speed of lightening.

Over the years, quite a lot of information has come to me this way, usually in the form of prose, but sometimes in rhyme. I would like to take credit for writing it, but I'm not sure I can. I wonder if it's even ethical to put my name to it. Then again, whose name could be put to it?

I wrote down the lines that came to me on sheets or little pieces of paper and then filed them away in various places, not knowing what I would ever do with them, just feeling that I might have a future use for them. I wish I had filed them more carefully because I can locate only a few of them today. Perhaps someday I will be able to get them all together and publish them in my next book. (Yes, I do hope I will someday write another book.)

At this point, I'd like to share with you some of the poetry and prose that came to me this way. Sometimes when I go back and read them, I am amazed and say to myself, "Did I write that?"

## POINT OF VIEW

When you have lost your money, home and all,

I say, "Surely, the Lord won't let you fall."

But when loss comes to me, with debts so deep,

Life is so unfair; all I can do is weep.

When I see you are feeling sick, I say,

"Now we must just let the Lord have His way."

But when I am in pain and really ill,

I say, "No, this cannot be Heaven's will."

When I see you all stricken down with grief,

I say, "Just you wait; God will give relief."

But when I am sad and no hope do I feel,

I say, "Oh, these tribulations are real."

It's so easy to give answers to you,

And explain exactly what you must do.

But when bad luck and trouble come to me,

My future is so dark and frightening to see.

## MY NEIGHBOR'S LAWN

Lord, why did you make my neighbor's lawn across the way

So plush and green, more beautiful than I can say?

Please just take a look at what you've done with my lawn.

How can you be so unfair, the grass practically all gone?

You know, dear Lord, just how much and how hard I pray

That you would make my lawn a place for angels to play;

Even more beautiful than any other lawn in sight;

A place where everything would be so perfect and right.

You know I'm good, dear Lord, praying to you all the time.

And what's my neighbor doing? But out spreading more lime!

While I'm with you, doing so right and praying so hard,

Where's my neighbor? But out there again toiling in his yard.

Can you see him there, lugging fertilizer all around?

And then spreading more grass seed over the ground.

Tugging, sweating and pulling that long garden hose

Always spraying more water in hope that it grows.

But, I so faithful, dear lord, have gone directly to you.

With all my trust, because I want only the best you can do.

I'm so patient, waiting for you to paint my lawn green

All manicured and trimmed the prettiest to be seen.

Please, dear Lord, I know some day you'll answer my prayer.

Maybe if I just pray harder, you'll show me you care.

## SINCE YOU HAVE GONE

In my mind I see you so clearly.

In my heart I love you so dearly.

I'm with you much more than you know

Even though I left so long ago.

My earth and yours are the same but not.

And time and space do not count a lot.

Our souls are joined together it seems.

Never will we part not even in dreams.

Together we will always be as one

'Til eternity ends and God's work is done.

# OR SO I TGHOUGHT

The best way to win an argument is to crush your adversary.

I am a better person than the other person,

If others don't like me, that is their problem.

Everyone likes me because I am very nice.

I can always apologize sometime in the future for what I just did.

Prayer is best for weaker people.

A soft answer turneth not away wrath.

I would be happy if I just had money.

People are nice to me because they like me.

Some people are just not worth bothering with.

I will never have time to accomplish what I want to do.

I have achieved much more in this life than you have.

I have not been put on Earth to help you with your problems

There is no end to my miseries.

When you are ill, that is of no concern to me.

# CODED MESSAGES

Reflect upon the following coded messages. Understanding will come to you as to how they apply to you and how you can improve conditions in your life. Consider that the more non-sensible in appearance, the greater the thought that must be given and the greater the potential.

Open your mouth before putting something into it.

Close your mouth before you speak.

Watch for when time is up.

Up can be down and down can be somewhere else.

Delay brings naught but patience brings everything.

Generosity begets generosity but not always.

Wisdom comes to those who listen but less to those who speak.

Meaning is given to those who seek it.

Boomerangs come back to you.

You can run away from what appears inevitable.

Put yourself before others and the soul is enflamed.

Heed not that which should not be heeded.

Insidious remarks have insidious results.

Destruction comes before noon.

Obsessions are obsessive.

Possessions are possessive.

Confessions delight the soul.

The edge of insanity has purpose.

# INSPIRATIONAL THOUGHTS

## Creating our future

When we think about our future, we often wonder just where our life's journey will take us. Let us never think of ourselves as the pawns of our destiny. Instead of wondering where our life's journey will take us, let us focus on where we will take our life's journey. Let us be aware that it is we alone who are the planners of our life's journey. We map our future with each and every action we make. We map our future with each and every word we say. We map our future with each and every thought we have. From this day forth, let each of us strive to plan a happy, pleasant journey for ourselves.

## From the past to the future

The time that we call "now" is the present. But it is really the past. Everything that we are experiencing at this time, whether it brings us pain or joy, is the result of our past thoughts and actions. We are living our past. The time that we call "now" is the present but it is really the future. Every thought we have right now, and every action we take, determine our future. We are living our future. We can't change the present. It was determined in the past. We can change our future. It is being determined right now.

## Time

Time has no beginning. Each day, each hour, each minute, each second is the end. The end of the past. There is no past. Each day, each hour, each minute, each second is the beginning. The beginning of the future. There is no future. Each day, each hour, each minute, each second Is the present. There is no present. Each day, each hour, each minute, each second is the beginning and the end. The end of the past. The beginning of the future. There is no time.

## The gift of time

Time is the gift of opportunities, the essence of the dimensions through which humans progress. Time is a sequence of opportunities. Humans evolve through their reactions to the opportunities that are presented to them. Time exists without measurement at the non-physical levels. Wasted time is missed opportunities.

## Our free will

Our creator has given a free will to each soul that has been created. As we exercise this free will, we carve out our own unique path to our spiritual destiny. With our every thought, our every word, and our every deed, the spiritual path that we must follow is created and laid out before us. Each soul enters this physical life equipped with a unique set of tools, specially selected to help us proceed down the spiritual path that we ourselves have created.

## individual differences

As we look at the people around us, we can see a great variety of individual differences. It is those differences that are the tools we possess to help us make progress on our spiritual journeys. They can be our race, our color, our health, our talents our intelligence level, our physical appearance, our strengths, our weaknesses, and a host of other kinds of differences, including whether we enter physical life as a man or as a woman.

## A greater meaning

Search for greater meaning in our lives. Seek increased awareness of the potential that lies within. Seek to nurture the spark of the divine that lies at the very core of our being. Achieve greater awareness of our true self. Think of ourselves as more than just our physical bodies and that which is perceived by our senses. Think of ourselves as more than just our feelings, our desires and our emotions. Think of ourselves as more than just our intellect, our reasoning and our thoughts. Know ourselves for that which we truly are: the creation of God, formed in the image of God with the seed of all of the attributes of our creator.

## Stolen memories

Childhood is a time of innocence, filled with enthusiasm and pleasure. It is a time of play with very few responsibilities. All your needs are taken care of by others. You live in the now and there are no worries about your future. Your past does not exist. Each day is a new lifetime for you, filled with excitement and an unending opportunity for new experiences. Time is endless, no need for you to think about yesterday or tomorrow. You feel loved. You are the center of the universe. This is how childhood is meant to be. These should be the memories of childhood. However, this is not how all childhoods are. The childhood memories have been stolen because such childhoods never existed.

## Spiritual adulthood

Grow a little closer toward spiritual adulthood. Understand that spiritual adulthood means having a full awareness of ourselves. Awareness of both the human aspects and of the spark of the divine within us leads us to oneness with our creator. Seek to learn more about our attitudes and our emotions so that we might grow in spirit.

As we seek greater understanding of ourselves, we cease being slaves to our emotions. Learn to become the masters of our feelings and attitudes. Know that through prayer, the direct communication link to our creator, we can bring great change into our lives.

When we find ourselves in the midst of unpleasant personal situations; when we find that things in our lives are not as we want them to be; when we desperately want things affecting our lives to change--then may we know that there is something better to do than praying for conditions affecting us to change. Instead of praying for our life's problems to go away, first learn to pray for a change in our emotions and attitudes toward those problems.

## The earthly kingdoms

Seek to enrich our awareness of the relationship between our creator, ourselves, and the planet on which we live. As our consciousness expands, we come to more fully understand that all of creation is in unity. All that exists in our dimension has been created for the benefit and for the development of the souls of mankind.

As we grow in spirituality, the mysteries of the interrelationships between each element of God's creation can be understood more clearly. The wondrous relationship between the earthly kingdoms of the mineral, the vegetable, and the animal all unite to work in unison. All placed in our presence to be used for our holy benefit.

Each kingdom has been designed and created to work in harmony with the human race. Pause to reflect that everything in our universe has been divinely created in perfect harmony, to be used by each one of us for the development of our eternal souls.

## Contribute positive

Recognize the positive and dwell upon it. For as we think positive, then do we contribute positive. If each one of us would contribute our portion of positive to our own small world around us, then the whole world will become more positive; more and more positive each day. Work for the spread of good. God is good. Let God be experienced throughout the world.

## A greater awareness

Be ever mindful that we are the creation of the divinity and have that spark of the divine within us. We are destined to learn and to grow, destined to fulfill the purpose for which we were created. Seek greater awareness of ourselves and the role that we are to play.

## Channelers

Let us become channels of kindness by showing kindness to those around us. Let us channel forgiveness by forgiving those whom we feel have offended us. Let us channel patience to all by being patient with all in all that we do. Let us channel God's love by thinking with love, speaking with love, and acting with love as we live from minute to minute, day to day, year to year and lifetime to lifetime.

## Children of God

We truly are children of God, formed in the image of God, created to be like God, destined to be one with God. That is a destiny we cannot avoid. We must arrive there. We can make it easy for ourselves or we can make it difficult. The choice is there. But that is our destiny. God has so ordained.

## Spiritual paths

There are many spiritual paths, each taking the traveler in the direction he should go; each leading to the same end and each seeking greater closeness to our Creator

## The human body

The human body is truly the magnificent, divine expression that has been given to us by our creator for our stay here on this earth. The human body enables each soul to express itself in this dimension as we fulfill our role in the divine plan for which we have been created.

## Our adversaries

Each individual in our circles of acquaintances has been created for the purpose of playing a role in the divine plan that our creator has given to us. Let us open our eyes to look around ourselves and take pleasure in appreciating the miracle of all that is wonderful and good in our lives.

Let us also experience the miracle of learning to be thankful for all that which does not seem so good and wonderful in our lives. Our adversaries, our enemies; our problems, our heartaches; our trials and tribulations are all here for good reason.

They are all necessary to us. It is they who are our teachers. It is they who provide us with opportunities to master the lessons needed to help us grow in spirit. As we learn from our teachers we grow in spirit and play the divine role for which we have been created.

## Healing

Healing of the body. Healing of the mind. Healing of the spirit. Let us be healed so that we may heal others. Let us heal others so that we may heal ourselves. For as we heal others, we heal ourselves. Healing is a kind thought. Healing is a kind word. Healing is a kind deed. Let us live, eat and breathe thoughts, words and deeds of kindness from this day forth. All that we do with only thoughts of ourselves is selfish and unkind. All that we do with kindness and thoughts of others creates healing. We have been created to be healers. Let us do that for which we were created. Let us heal. Let us begin this very moment.

## Our needs

What if we tried to become like the man who said, "I am indeed the richest man on earth because I live my life so that my needs are few."? What if we looked within and could see all our greed? What if we saw that our wants become our needs, and the more we get, the more we want, the more we need?

We have created a life of unending needs. So we never achieve our original goal. We never experience true inner satisfaction. As we withhold satisfaction from ourselves, we make it so that we can never experience the peace that comes from satisfying our needs.

What if we were to realize that external needs are really very few in number? What if we concentrated on our inner needs, the needs of the spirit? As we satisfy our inner needs, we achieve inner peace. True riches are those that lie within us.

## Part Four

# ABOUT THE PENDULUM

## What the pendulum does

A significant approach to elevating the overall level of humanity is to lower the level of stress in peoples' lives. The use of the pendulum presents an excellent opportunity to do that. The pendulum will give answers to questions by the questioner. Receiving the answers to many questions will reduce the tendency for the individual to worry, thus reducing stress. In a less stressful society the world will be much different from the world we now know.

## How to word a question

The questions asked of the pendulum must be designed to elicit responses that can be either yes or no. Interrogative words (who, what, when, where, how, why how many etc.) cannot begin a question. To receive answers to those types of questions a series of questions that include suggested possible answers can be asked until a yes or no response is given. For example, instead of asking What will the weather be tomorrow?, instead ask such questions as Will it rain tomorrow? Will it be cold tomorrow?, Will it be overcast tomorrow? etc. until the desired response is given.

## Making a pendulum

Simply take a piece of string (or thin wire, jewelry chain etc.) six inches or longer and tie a small weight such as a key or anything else you choose onto one of the ends. Heavier weights and longer strings often provide a more obvious response. Then hold the string upright by the other end between the thumb and forefinger.

## Understanding the response of the pendulum

As you hold the string upright between your thumb and forefinger say Show me your yes and the weight will move in one of three different directions, either from right to left, or to and from you, or in a circular motion. It varies from person to person. For the author a yes answer is indicated by a back and forth movement; a no answer by a movement to and from him; and a clockwise circular movement usually means sometimes yes sometimes no or sometimes this and sometimes that and a counterclockwise means there is no answer to be given at this time. He sometimes finds that a no answer starts out as a yes answer and then changes direction into a no answer. Likewise on other occasions a yes answer will start out as no answer. When this occurs, it indicates that there is only a little difference between the yes and the no. So let the weight swing a while to make sure it doesn't change directions.

## Asking a question

To ask a question, just hold the string upright between the thumb and forefinger at the very end of the non-weighted end, ask the question and wait for the answer. Actually just thinking the question is usually enough but some may find it preferable to say the question out loud. The only word of caution is that you shouldn't ask any questions for which you are not emotionally prepared to hear an answer you don't want to hear. The more you use the pendulum, the more proficient you will become. Don't abandon the pendulum if you are not successful with it after just a few attempts. It will likely take many experiences with the pendulum to become very proficient.

## Testing or validating the responses of pendulum

You can validate the response by of the pendulum by asking the same question but worded differently so that the opposite answer would be expected. (Will it rain today? Will today be rain free?)

(Will the questioner's emotions affect the response given by the pendulum? Will the questioner's emotions not affect the response?)

## About the pendulum

The pendulum receives information from the level immediately above the soul level: the higher self level. If you just think of a question instead of saying it aloud, the response of the pendulum will be the same.

When questions are asked about a person's future decisions, the answer may not always be 100 percent accurate because it will be based on the outcomes the exercise of free will on his previous actions in similar situations in the past.

The extent and accuracy of the pendulum's responses depend on the user's higher self; that is "the elements and aspects of the soul that are necessary for the current incarnation".

The only reasons why a wrong answer is sometimes given:

1. There is interference from spirits.
2. The answer involves the exercise of free will.
3. The questioner's strong desire for a specific answer.

Wrong answers usually occur because of the interference of the spirits. Spirits have the ability to move objects and the pendulum is the easiest object to move. You can suspect spirit interference when the pendulum acts erratically after you ask a question. Ask the pendulum if there is spirit interference and if the answer is yes you can remove spirit interference if you say *"Spirit please leave while I am asking questions."* Then ask the pendulum again if there is spirit interference. The answer is almost always no.

The pendulum cannot always answer questions with 100% accuracy when they involve how you will exercise your free will (i.e. desires). If it could, then the will would not be unrestricted (free). The response will be predicted on how you responded in similar past situations.

Whether the answer is correct or incorrect, the pendulum will always give the same answer to the same question.

If you want to be somewhat sure, after an answer say *"Was the answer to the question just asked correct (or incorrect)?"* You could also say *"Were the answers to the last 2 (3, 4, 5 etc.) questions correct (or incorrect)?"*

The pendulum will answer any question asked, regardless of how ridiculous, disrespectful, opinionated, etc. it is.

When another person asks a question that is heard by the user of the pendulum, the pendulum receives the question through the user's mind. Although the user can repeat the question aloud, it is not necessary to do so. The pendulum receives the question from the mind of the user, indirectly from the mind of the questioner.

The source of the pendulum's receiving the questions (not the answers) from the questioner is not the person's conscious mind, but rather the subconscious mind. All conscious thoughts come through the subconscious mind. Therefore the wording of the question does not necessarily have to be precise. Even wrong words thought by the questioner do not matter.

The source of the pendulum's answers to questions is the questioner's higher self. Once again, the higher self can be defined as the elements and aspects of the soul that are necessary for the current incarnation. The higher self of the questioner communicates with the higher self of the pendulum user.

Questions can be answered over the when the questioner asks the question or even just thinks the question. For some questions it may be preferable that the user not know the question.

The pendulum can also enable a proficient user to communicate with specific spirits simply holding the pendulum and thinking of the spirit. The communication is limited because they can respond only to questions which ask for a yes/no answer.

As previously stated, receiving the answers to many questions will reduce the tendency for the individual to worry, thus reducing stress. In a less stressful society the world will be much different from the world we now know.

## Part Five

# EXPLANATION OF TERMS

Information about the major people mentioned in this book is located in the chapter titled *Personalities.*

**Alliance**

The Alliance, otherwise known as the Elohim, is the positive force that works for the benefit of mankind as opposed to the negative force referred to as the Cabal. Elohim is a plural word. According to www.biblestudytools.com/bible-study/ the term "Elohim" means "supreme one" or "mighty one." It is not only used of the one true God but is also used on occasion to refer to human rulers, judges, and even angels.

**Antichrists**

Antichrists are humans whose goal is to impede the development of humanity, the opposite of the role of Christs.

**Anunnaki**

The Anunnaki are extraterrestrials from a different planet in our solar system. They have been instrumental in the evolution of Earth humans.

**Ark of the Covenant**

The Ark of the Covenant contained alien technology for defending the Jews in Biblical times.

## Astral world

The astral world is another term for the spirit world. Every planet or moon inhabited by humans or humanoids has an astral world.

## Atlantis

Atlantis was a continent about the size of Western Europe that existed in the North Atlantic Ocean until about 11,000 years ago. An earthquake caused it to shift and become what is now the continent of Antarctica.

## Book of Enoch

The Book of Enoch was found among the Dead Sea Scrolls in 1947. It includes much information about the Jews that is not in the Bible.

## Cabal

According to the dictionary the Cabal is " **the contrived schemes of a group of persons secretly united in a plot (as to overturn a government) also**: a group engaged in such schemes." The Cabal is an umbrella type of "organization". It includes the Deep State, the One World Order, and the Luciferians etc. It is the negative force opposed the positive force called the Alliance.

## Ceres

Ceres is a very small dwarf planet within the asteroid belt.

## Christs

Christs are spirits who have reached a level of evolution where reincarnation is no longer necessary but who have voluntarily chosen to reincarnate for the purpose of helping and elevating the consciousness of mankind. They have not yet reached a level of perfection.

## Christ spirits

Christ spirits are spirits that have evolved to the point that reincarnation is no longer necessary. They are not perfect and must continue their evolution in the spirit world. If they so wish, they can reincarnate to enhance their evolution. If they reincarnate to assist in the raising of consciousness of humanity they are called Christs.

## Etheric body

The etheric body connects the physical body and the spirit body by a silver cord. Pain is felt in the etheric body. When the silver cord is cut, death occurs.

## Evolution

Every individual, whether in the physical form or in the spirit form, is a creation of the soul. The soul is endlessly evolving by the information that is inputted into it by the human or by the spirit.

## Extraterrestrials

Extraterrestrials are human or humanoid beings whose home planet is anywhere other than Earth in the universe.

**Fallen angels**

Fallen angels are not angels, but were originally very tall inhabitants of the planet Jupiter who disobeyed orders when they mated with Earth people whose offspring were called the Nephilim.

**Free will**

Every soul is endowed with free will. This is the capacity to have desires. Since the will is free this means that only the person himself can change his desires although others can make it difficult or impossible to achieve those desires.

**Ghosts**

Ghosts are spirits who are caught in the in-between world and have not completed their passage from the physical world to the spirit world.

**Grays**

The Grays are a humanoid race of extraterrestrials that look like the typical portrayal of non-Earth beings, with large eyes, a large bald head and a rather puny body. They could be the human race of the future.

**Higher self**

The higher self is the elements and aspects of the soul which are necessary for the current incarnation. This is the deepest level of consciousness that can be accessed by the individual.

## Holy Spirit

The Holy Spirit is the highest level of spirit that could dwell in the human body along with the human's ego.

## Homonoeticus

The Homonoeticus are new race of more highly evolved humans which will eventually replace Homosapiens in approximately 100,000 years.

## Human

Humans are Earth people and the 98 percent of all extraterrestrials who look exactly like us.

## Humanoid

Two percent of extraterrestrials look similar to how science fiction shows them. All humanoids have the same basic shape; that is, a torso, two arms, two legs, a neck and head. Many are not covered in skin as are Earth people, but rather is leather, scales, feathers etc.

## Hybrid race

Humans of a hybrid race are part human from one extraterrestrial group and part extraterrestrial human from a different extraterrestrial group. All Earth humans are hybrids.

## Illuminati

The Illuminati are a division of the Cabal.

## In-between world

The in-between world is a place between the physical world and the spirit world that is the home of those who have died but have not yet fully crossed over to the spirit world. It is where ghosts dwell.

## Indigo children

Indigo children are brilliant, intelligent and very superior star children who are quite mystical.

## Karma

Karma is simply a case of cause and effect. For every thought, word or deed there is an equal and opposite reaction that a person experiences, whether positive or negative, whether in this lifetime or in another.

## Lemuria

Lemuria was an ancient continent in the Pacific Ocean that predated Atlantis. The Hawaiian Islands were once part of Lemuria.

## Luciferians

The Luciferians are a faction of the Cabal.

## Masters

There are 73 masters who are in charge of the development of all entities in both the physical world and the spirit world.

## Medium

A Medium is a person that has direct communication with those in the spirit world.

## Mental world

After an entity no longer has a need to reincarnate and resides in the spirit world, they eventually move on to a higher level than the spirit world; what Theosophists call the mental world.

## Nephilim giants

Nephilim giants are the offspring of tall humans from Jupiter and Earth humans. Goliath in the Bible was one of them. Most were destroyed in the Great Flood.

## New Age

The New Age is a philosophical movement created by the channelings of Helena Blavatsky and others in the nineteenth century. Their work created the body of knowledge referred to as Theosophy.

## Niburu

Niburu is a very distant planet in our solar system about twenty times further away from the sun than Neptune. It approaches the earth once every 5000 years and when it does so, much disturbance is created on the planet and its inhabitants.

## One World Order

The One World order is a division of the Cabal which seeks to create a one world government with all the power concentrated at the top of the hierarchy.

## Priory of Sion

The Priory of Sion is an ancient society which attempts to prove that Jesus had offspring whose descendants who became the Merovingian kings if France.

## Reincarnation

Reincarnation is the process by which the soul creates a new body for an individual to be born again for another lifetime after having spent many years in the spirit realm.

## Soul

The soul is the essence of the individual. It is what distinguishes one person from another. It is dynamic, forever evolving by means of what humans and spirits input into it by their thoughts, words and deeds. The God force dwells in the soul and animates it.

## Spirit

The soul creates both the human form and the spirit form of the entity. The soul and the spirit are not synonymous.

## Spirit guide

We each have a spirit guide who stays with us throughout our life to protect and guide us. This is primarily done by projecting thoughts telepathically into our minds that we believe are our own thoughts. They also project thoughts into the minds of others who wish to harm us.

## Spirit world

After we die we continue to exist in the spirit world where all who have died reside except those who have left for another incarnation in the physical world.

## Split Soul

When a person has both his own spirit dwelling in his body and also another spirit simultaneously, that is referred to as a split soul. This can occur for a limited amount of time, or for the life of the person.

## Star child

Star children are the forerunners of a new race of humans, the Homonoeticus, which will eventually replace Homosapiens who will be more evolved.

## Stargate

Stargates are places in our planet where people can go through a portal and emerge in faraway places in the universe and also go into the future and into the past. Also known as wormholes.

## Sumer

An ancient civilization in what is now southern Iraq. The Sumerian civilization produced many stone tablets with ancient writings about prehistoric times.

## Theosophy

Theosophy was created by Helena Blavatsky in the late nineteenth century along with several other individuals. It is a belief system which is credited as the beginning of the New Age movement.

## Tiamat

Tiamat was once a planet between Mars and Jupiter that broke up into many particles that became what is known as the asteroid belt.

## Walk-ins/Walkouts

A walk-out is when a person, for various reasons, wishes to go back to the spirit world and allow another spirit to take over his body until it dies. A walk-in is the spirit which takes over the body.

## Watchers

From the Book of Enoch, the watchers are often called fallen angels; but they were actually tall human beings from Jupiter who mated with humans. The offspring of the mating were ten foot tall giants called the Nephilim.

Printed in the United States
by Baker & Taylor Publisher Services